Love
Metabolism

A GUIDE TO TURNING UP THE HEAT IN YOUR RELATIONSHIP

the Three Keys
to Fully Satisfying
All Your
Relationship Needs

GINA GUDDAT MA, LMHC & RAY ANDERSON MA, LMHC

Love Metabolism

This book is dedicated to Ben and Nadine Rogers,
who have been happily married for 60 years.

Is there a better example of two people who have learned each other's "love metabolism"? At age 81 and 90, they still hold hands and kiss in public, share a cup of coffee each morning, and take daily walks together. From engaging in deep conversations to watching football games, they thoroughly enjoy each other's company. Thank you for being an example to us and so many others. Love truly can last a lifetime!

CONTENTS

INTRODUCTION

Love Metabolism—Food for Thought

Love "metabolism"? That's right—*love metabolism*! Allow us to explain. The phrase just struck us one day while discussing hot topics in couples counseling. We were consulting about the plight of one of our clients. He was having difficulties meeting the needs of his significant other, and it occurred to us that people seemingly burn through "love calories" in the same way their bodies burn through *food* calories. There it was! The concept that love, itself, has its own metabolism. But before we get into the meat of it, let's properly set the table for discussion. This frustrated client's story (we'll call him "Chris") goes something like this:

Chris was trying to finish a long phone conversation with his partner (we'll call her "Jessica") during his drive home. Once again, a simple, daily debriefing took a turn for the worse. This time, the problem started when Chris announced that he had invited a male friend to join them the next Sunday at their favorite restaurant to watch an NFL football game (and to think he was *so* close—maybe a minute or two away—to ending the call unscathed!). No sooner did the words leave his mouth then Jessica produced a long sigh—and then a long list of all the people and obligations that had made their demands on their "together time" over the previous couple of weekends. She lamented the idea that, once again, they would be looking at a weekend filled with other people and other things.

But why was she so disappointed, Chris wondered? Why the agitation over such a small thing? These questions loomed as he listened to her bemoan the prospect of yet another "wash of a weekend." What did that mean, anyway? A "wash," as in neither good nor bad? As in the entire weekend coming to naught? *Really*? As Chris saw things, they were about to have virtually the entire weekend to themselves, minus half a day celebrating her father's birthday on Saturday and a few hours of football on Sunday. In truth, they would be together the entire time, just not *alone* together. Didn't that count for something? It wasn't as though Jessica didn't enjoy hanging out with other people and Chris at the same time. On the contrary, Jessica had amazing social dexterity; she was the kind of woman who could entertain guests, juggle five different text threads, and still make him feel like he was the most important person in the room.

Yet there she was complaining, suggesting, perhaps, that she didn't feel he valued her enough—that he didn't give her enough of his time or energy. Chris was confused and even a little offended. Did they not just spend 10 straight days together in late December, six of those skiing on a romantic get-away? Did they not just dress to the nines on New Year's Eve and dance the night away as a couple? And yet not three weekends later, Jessica was accusing him of failing to put her front and center on his calendar! To be fair, Chris acknowledged that the previous two weekends were a bit busy with family obligations and entertaining. All-in-all, though, he felt they were having a pretty nice month as a couple. As far as Chris was concerned, he *had* put her front and center!

So what was Jessica *really* saying, then? As the conversation dragged on, it was growing more and more difficult to tell. By the end of the call, her complaints weren't nearly as loud as the raucous clicking of Chris' own defensive triggers. It wasn't until later the next day, after some time to cool down and carefully reflect on their conversation, that Chris began to see things more clearly. What he realized was that Jessica was not, in fact, accusing him of being selfish with his time or complaining that she didn't feel loved or valued enough. It only sounded that way. What she actually communicated was that in spite of all the time they had recently spent alone together, she was ready for more. Put another way, she was telling Chris she was *hungry* . . . which brings us full circle to the title of our book.

Love Metabolism! While comparing affairs of the heart to matters of the stomach may seem strange, allow us to chew on the metaphor for a moment. Indeed, Jessica *was* hungry; the troubled timbre of her voice was only the sound of an unsatisfied appetite. Never mind that she had just feasted on their recent holiday "together time," as Chris did. Forget the fact that over 10 long days, they had sampled, snacked, and even binged a few times—just the two of them. In the end, it mattered little. She wanted more. She *needed* more.

So what's the underlying problem, here, from a love-metabolic perspective? Simply put, their metabolic rates weren't in synch. Jessica had burned up the entire supply of love energy she had consumed two weeks before. Chris, on the other hand, was still happily digesting. Think of it as a scene on Thanksgiving Day a few hours after dinner: The man—one hand struggling to undo his belt and the other caressing his gut—blissfully descends into holiday oblivion in his oversized recliner, while the woman of the house, having burned more calories cooking and cleaning than she consumed from a modest helping of turkey and mashed potatoes, proudly informs her guests that it's time to enjoy her tasty, homemade pies! Now, we don't mean to suggest that ten days together over the holidays was enough to put Chris into some kind of relationship food coma. But the truth is, he was still quite full, even after a couple weeks! A little bit of quality time together goes a long way for him. Chris' love metabolism is characterized by a slow, sustained burn, if you will. Jessica's love metabolism is vastly different. For her, two weeks without concentrated, one-on-one quality time might as well be a seven-year famine. In short, Chris stores—and Jessica burns.

And there you have it! That's how we cooked up the concept of *love metabolism*. We sincerely hope the metaphor is as delicious to you as it is to us. Admittedly, we might be having a little too much fun with the wordplay, but we think you'll find that looking at love through a metabolic lens will help you see your relationship from a completely new perspective. In the following pages, you will begin to understand that success in love is not simply a matter of identifying *what* is needed; it is equally a matter of determining how *often*, how *long*, and how *much*!

Unlocking and applying these three, love-metabolic keys will help you create your own culinary masterpiece—a tried-and-true recipe for lasting love that quiets the hunger and leads to years of satisfaction and fulfillment.

Happy reading—and bon appétit!

An Important Note to Our Readers:

In our two practices as mental health counselors, we feel privileged to have worked with a wide variety of couples. Based on that work, we know that circumstances shape the issues that couples face. Established couples face different challenges than those just starting out, for example. And couples who have children face issues unique to parenting. Still, we believe that the principles of *Love Metabolism* apply to everyone. Seeking to understand each other better—and to work to meet each other's needs—naturally will help any couple.

That said, the examples cited in the book feature heterosexual couples. That's a decision we reached only after careful consideration. It's simply an acknowledgement that the unique issues faced by same-sex couples warrant a rich exploration. We're unable to do justice to that exploration within the limitations of this book, and believe it would be disrespectful to present anything less. We appreciate your understanding.

PART I

CHAPTER 1

The Heart Yearns as Calories Burn

We hear it all too often: A relationship comes to a frustrating end because one feels that the other can't "meet my needs." In other cases, it's because one feels that the other is "too needy." But do these generalizations tell the whole story? Is it really possible to reduce the reasons for relational failure to such sweeping and simplistic reasoning? We say, "no." To do so is to ignore the complexities inherent in human relationships. It is far more accurate to say that relationships often end because couples fail to identify very specific needs or, if they do, they stop short of learning how to meet them *fully*. This second possibility—that needs are sometimes identified, but not met fully—is where our book and the concept of love metabolism come in.

Let's say that Jennifer and Jon have been married for many years and that Jon has learned the hard way that his wife needs a lot of communication. Since making the discovery, he has done his utmost to keep a continual line of communication open with Jennifer. He calls her for a few minutes every day from his office, once during his mid-morning coffee break and again when he leaves for the day. Then, when he arrives at home, he takes a moment to engage her in conversation, usually sharing some menial details about his work day and occasionally adding some mildly entertaining gossip about co-workers. In his own short-sighted way, Jon feels satisfied that he is doing a good job staying in touch, a fact that makes it all the more perplexing when Jennifer complains that she isn't getting enough from him.

See, for Jennifer, the problem isn't that Jon doesn't communicate enough with her. Since they first confronted the problem several years back, Jennifer has noticed Jon's efforts to reach out more and initiate communication. She is actually satisfied with the number of calls and chats. Then again, that's all they are to her: Little calls and little chats. In the end, she finds herself hungry for more, but "more" for Jennifer has nothing to do with quantity. Jennifer is tired of brief, shallow banter with her husband. For once, she would love to get lost in a long conversation, the kind that holds her interest captive and makes the hours pass away like minutes. More than this, however, Jennifer craves substance! She wants to descend below the surface and explore topics that will challenge them to think, expand their understanding of each other, and deepen their love. In short, Jennifer feels they are communicating—but not *connecting*.

In metabolic terms, Jennifer and Jon have identified a specific need (regular communication), but their appetites for that need are very different. Jon is fine with a bite, a nibble. A snack here and there matches his slower love metabolism. Jennifer, on the other hand, is left seriously undernourished and underwhelmed by the appetizers Jon is offering her. Snacking is acceptable some of the time, sure, but she desperately needs an occasional sit-down, full-course meal with a lot of communication calories. Without it, she inevitably feels a rumble in her gut that tells her she simply isn't getting enough sustenance!

LOVE METABOLISM AND F.I.D.

Let's look at Jon and Jennifer's differences another way, by comparing our concept of love metabolism to a conceptual model widely used in the health and fitness industry: F.I.D. (frequency, intensity, duration). The Aerobic and Fitness Association of America (AFAA), the American Council on Exercise (ACE), and the National Strength and Conditioning Association (NSCA), among others, uniformly subscribe to the F.I.D. model as a way to measure the effectiveness of any given workout routine. Most of us know by now that the average person is encouraged to engage in aerobic activity from three to five days per week, for a minimum of 20 to 60 minutes, with a heart rate that falls within 55-85% of your maximum beats per minute. That's F.I.D. in a nutshell! You have frequency (three to five days), intensity (55-85%), and duration (20 to 60 minutes). Of course, what is appropriate in all three areas depends on the person. Athletes need to be challenged. They consume and expend a lot of calories per day and must actively manipulate F.I.D. to make gains. If you're an average, out-of-shape adult, a kid, or a senior, you will only be able to push yourself so much. A little tweak here and there in F.I.D. should be enough. If you're suffering from a nagging injury, then you really need to be careful with F.I.D. Too much, too long, too often could be detrimental to your physical health and overall well-being.

And so it is with love and relationships! Applying the concept of love metabolism, the key to fulfilling an identified need is to get the frequency, intensity, and duration right. Too much at one time—or too little—misses the mark. Just often enough, for the right amount of time, hits the target. It's all about the balance. Make no mistake, it takes a lot of time in the "workout room of the heart" to get in tune with your partner's needs. There are as many needs—and they can change according to circumstances—as there are ways to satisfy them. It takes a steady, methodical approach—the same kind of mindset needed to get into great physical shape! But when you finally "learn" your partner and know how to successfully apply F.I.D. to the needs in your relationship, the rewards are incredible—rewards measured not in pounds lost or muscle gained, but rather in the increase of love, intimacy, and emotional safety. Keep reading! With the information in our book and some sweat on your part, you'll have a real shot at becoming a bona fide relationship "athlete"!

So while good things lay ahead, let's look at things as they *really* are. If you're like the rest of us, you haven't yet learned how to *fully* satisfy at least some of your partner's needs. Now, in a perfect world, your partner is someone whose overall love metabolism closely matches yours. But let's face it, how many of us consider such things when choosing a mate? Personality type, family of origin, culture, and past experience with relationships, among other factors, all combine to shape a person's appetite for intimacy in all its various forms. With that in mind, landing someone with a similar background and appetite is, in theory, a real bonus. But that's just theory, and we live in the real world of imperfect people and imperfect choices. What can two people do, then, when their discrepancies in background and appetites begin to surface and cause tension in their relationship? It's a question we'll be answering in detail throughout the book.

LOVE METABOLISM AND OUR TIMES

Speaking of tension, Jon and Jennifer's relationship problems may seem a product of their own doing, but in fact they may also be caused in part by recent societal and cultural developments occurring world-wide. See, Jon and Jennifer belong to an ever-expanding, social media-driven world that has its citizens more connected than ever before. Yet many of its citizens have never felt so locally *isolated*. We live in a world in which Jennifer might send 25 texts a day to friends around the country but has never found the time to meet her neighbors next door. It's a place in which Jon can instantly download all the movies he wants and watch them in the comfort of his own home, while the friends he used to meet up with to catch the latest movie on opening weekend have all gradually lost touch with one another. In short, we have never been able to "go" so many places and do so many things without so much as opening our front door.

The truth is the world of social media and mass communication is expanding while the traditional and tangible model of the neighborly "village" is shrinking. That reality comes with an ironic twist—and a price. While outlets for communication seem endless, people are placing their hopes for physical, emotional, and spiritual happiness in the hands of fewer and fewer "live" people. Esther Perel, author of the best-selling book, *Mating in Captivity*, speaks to this social phenomenon occurring around the world. She noted that as societies grow more and more individualistic, couples increasingly rely on their romantic partnerships to meet most of their social and emotional needs—needs that used to be met through regular interaction with a variety of family members, friends, and neighbors.

What "used to be" actually wasn't all that long ago, as a matter of fact. Those of us enjoying our middle adulthood remember those broken-record grandparents who continually mourned the loss of a bygone era when life was simpler and the world hadn't yet gone to "hell in a hand basket." Their generation is as far back as you need to travel to illustrate how much the social fabric has changed. If Jennifer and Jon had met in the 1950s, for example, the expectations they had for one another might have been significantly limited, by comparison. It's not that they wouldn't have possessed the same highly personalized appetites and expectations as modern-day couples, but rather that they would have been much more likely to consider other key social outlets as equally important sources for fulfillment.

Our grandparents' world wasn't filled with Costco, Amazon, or Super Wal-Mart. It wasn't the world of see it all now, get it all now. Theirs was a culture defined by the *five and dime* corner store, a compartmentalized consumer landscape that required time and patience to navigate. On any given day, for example, our 1950s Jennifer might run to the jeweler to get her watch repaired, drop her shoes off at the cobbler, pop into the stationery store to get her parents an anniversary card, pull into the "service" station to watch eager attendants fill her gas tank, and scurry off to her friend's house for "bridge night," a weekly, therapeutic girls-only gathering. Meanwhile, Jon might be out for the evening attending a weekly gathering at the Elks club, competing with his buddies in bowling league, or chairing a committee meeting at his church. No, our 1950s Jon and Jennifer would have had no concept of the power of social media or the convenience of point-and-click shopping, but they would have been more likely to enjoy tightly-woven social support networks that met their diverse social and emotional needs.

But times change! Our Jon and Jennifer live in the here-and-now, and for them the time is *now* to make real changes—changes that will help them satisfy their hunger for love and fulfillment. If your story is at all like Jon and Jennifer's, our book will be a wealth of information to you. It will introduce you to the world of love metabolism and help you identify the metabolic gaps in your relationship—those needs that are identified but undernourished. If you're like Jon, for example, our book will help you to rise above your one-dimensional view of "communication" and recognize the more complex reality—that your problems are not related to the frequency of that communication, but rather to the intensity and duration. More specifically, you will learn that you need to occasionally engage in longer talks about deeper subjects.

Armed with that knowledge and sharpened self-awareness, you will then roll up your sleeves and do the work that all successful couples do to uncover each other's' needs and learn just *how* to meet them. Chapter by chapter, we will suggest specific ways to do just that! Stay tuned! You will also see a dedicated chapter at the end of the book designed to give you workable strategies to help you succeed. Don't worry—you *will* get your fill!

CHAPTER 2

Communication: What a Girl Wants . . . What a Guy Needs

How often do we hear this, whether from the professional perch of the therapist's chair or over a cup of coffee at Starbucks: "We just don't talk anymore," or "I just don't understand what she's saying half the time"? We could list a hundred other similar complaints here, but the one, desperate declaration that reverberates louder and more often than the others usually comes from the female camp: "I wish he would just communicate *more* with me!" If you're female, we can tell you with confidence that you need more words than men do—period! This is almost beyond debate, whether we cite findings from empirical studies on the subject or simply make an appeal to sheer common sense. If you've been on the planet for any length of time, you know this to be true. In fact, if you're holding this book, then chances are pretty good that you're female (either that, or your female partner is making you read it). When's the last time your man walked in and said, "Hey honey, I picked up a book that I hope will really help our relationship!"? Just by your very nature, you generally lean on words more than men. This is especially true if you are attempting to save or strengthen a relationship.

Question: Is it a bad thing that men need less verbal communication than women? Removing the gender lens for a moment, let's ask this another way: Is it bad that anyone prefers fewer words and a little more peace and quiet? Is it wrong to be an introvert? As absurd as these questions seem, there are many quiet and shy people out there who unfortunately feel pressure to be different. In truth, there is no right or wrong way to be. Talkative is not better than soft-spoken. Outgoing is not better than reserved. A shy couple has every chance of relational bliss as that life-of-the-party couple that holds everyone captive. The real issue here is one of love metabolism! A metabolic match is a match, no matter what side of the communication continuum you fall on.

But as romantic partners aren't usually the perfect metabolic match when it comes to sharing words with each other, they have to "learn the burn," as we call it. With time and patience, they learn how much to say, how often to say it, and how to make what they say matter. With that in mind, it seems that "learning the burn" is more difficult for men than it is women. Let's be honest: Not many men out there would complain that their weekend couples retreat could have gone so much better *if there had only been more talking*! In fact, men aren't likely to factor the amount of communication into their equation for measuring the quality of together-time. Instead, they might factor in other metabolic variables (FID) that are more important to them, such as the *quality* of those discussions. But then, men and women don't always perceive quality or quantity in the same ways, do they? A man might drive home from his couples weekend thinking, "Boy, that was fun talking about the great plays we've seen this season," while the woman sitting next to him is thinking, "I can't believe all we talked about was football!"

Feel hopeless sometimes? It's true that the gender communication gap can be frustrating and even maddening. Don't lose heart, though! Men and women are different when it comes to their hunger for words, for sure, but try to remember that your task is not to learn about *men and women*; your task is to learn about the person in front of you. What really matters is how well you know your romantic partner's unique love-metabolic needs for communication and what you do to act on that knowledge, something we'll focus on in the next chapter. For now, though, we think it's important and helpful to recognize a few truths regarding communication, gender, and love metabolism; there are definitely recurring themes worth mentioning when it comes to male/female communication misfires.

FOOD FOR THOUGHT: Women use around 20,000 words per day, while men average 7,000. Not surprisingly, women also speak faster than men do, (Louann Brizendine, M.D., *The Female Brain*, Harmony Books, 2007.)

WHAT A GIRL WANTS...

So, why do women burn through so many more communication calories than men do? Perhaps the reason is that women tend to use words—and lots of them—to *process and connect*. Many times, what women discuss is not nearly as therapeutic as the entire process of discussing it. Thus, articulating words—not so much the information words contain—is the medicine that heals. Men, on the other hand, are far more content-oriented. Sure, they get together with buddies on the weekend to banter about sports and share jokes from time to time, but information sharing and gathering is usually the central function of their communication. Remember that old expression, "Just the facts, ma'am"? That resonates with lots of guys, just as surely as it drives their female partners nuts.

Ladies, have you ever felt derailed when you're sharing some exciting news with your man and he turns your story into an interrogation? Perhaps this sounds familiar:

WOMAN: "Hey, I'm so excited to tell you I got a promotion at work! Can you believe it?"

MAN: "That is so cool. How did you end up getting it?"

WOMAN: "Well, I don't know exactly but I applied and they liked my interview. Can you believe it?"

MAN: "That's really cool. What's your new job description?"

WOMAN: "I'll be doing more marketing work than before and attending strategic meetings. I'm so happy!"

MAN: "What kinds of marketing work will you be doing? Will that take up most of your day do you think?"

WOMAN: (Ugh!!!)

And herein lies one of the most prevalent problems in male/female communication: Men often miss the point by assuming there has to be one! Please understand, we are not implying that women seldom have a point when communicating. Of course they do. It's just that men can become so myopically focused on information gathering (and its evil twin, advice-giving) that they misunderstand what women *really* need: An empathetic ear. In the dialogue above, the woman simply wants the man to share in the excitement of her story. Meanwhile, the man is attempting to show sincere interest by clarifying "the facts" of the story. What's she saying? Does it all add up? What does she want me to do about it? These are the kinds of questions swimming around in the male brain, while two better questions men might ask are, "Where is this conversation coming from and what does she need from me right now?"

Notice that we did not say, "What does she *need me to do?*" A woman's complaint that her man doesn't know how to listen often goes hand-in-hand with her gripe that he's always trying to "fix" her. Now, that's funny for the typical man to hear, because he could swear that somewhere in her dialogue is a plea for help with *something*. He's listening for the *thing* he needs to fix, while she becomes irritated by the sense that he sees *her* as the project. But for a man, it's usually anything but personal. Fixing anyone, let alone his romantic partner, likely never crosses his mind. That's far too daunting a project to even consider, with or without Home Depot. Still, that's the way it feels to her—personal. His goal is to express love by listening carefully and finding the solution, while her goal is to feel loved by being heard and understood. As you can see, these two goals just won't align because each has an entirely different premise for communication.

Men, as capable as you are—as clear-headed and solution-oriented as you may be in other roles—you need to flick off the switch to your problem-solver and open up the superhighway between your ears and heart. That's it! Now, that's not to say there aren't times when she really needs tangible solutions to real-life problems. But much of the time all she wants you to do is listen with compassion and reflect understanding. Remember, a woman that feels understood is a woman that probably feels loved, too.

There is a small, crucial window of opportunity when you can identify what she's really seeking—usually early in the conversation, before you're fully immersed in the details of her story. When you sense that window open to you, ask yourself, "What does it *feel* like she wants from this conversation?" Once you're in tune with the answer to *that* question, keep yourself in check through silent self-talk. Say to yourself, "Just listen. That's what she *really* needs right now. There's no problem here you need to fix. Put away the toolbox. If she needs a favor or an opinion, she'll ask." If you still aren't clear what her motives are, just ask her. We know of a man who is so emotionally confident and comfortable with his wife that he sometimes just comes right out and asks, "Hey, honey, is this one of those times when I should just sit back and listen?"

Un-phased, she usually replies with something like, "Yes, dear, it is. You can relax."

FOOD FOR THOUGHT: Romantic partners should never give unsolicited advice to one another, according to relationship guru John Gottman, Ph.D,. Instead, they should show genuine interest, offer affection and validate emotions. (*The Seven Principles for Making Marriage Work*, Harmony Books, 1999).

Once you learn how to resist the natural born urge to fix things, you're still not out of the woods. Surely your female companion appreciates the active listening and restraint on your part, but just because you listen with empathy doesn't mean you will express it correctly when it *is* time for you to respond. We're talking about a more subtle communication pitfall: *Minimizing*. It's something that haplessly rolls off men's tongues with the greatest of ease. Here are some of the more egregious examples:

"So your boss got mad at you *once*. Mine is upset every other day. You'll be fine."

"Yes, your friend said some things but I don't get why you were so upset with her."

"Well, you know how your mom is. I thought you didn't care what she thinks, anyway."

These statements don't exactly convey the type of understanding a woman is looking for, do they? They're pretty obvious. Other more nuanced examples of minimizing, however, demonstrate how easily a well-meaning man can go astray:

"Honey, that's really rough, but you shouldn't let it affect you. You're better than those people."

"Sure one person said *one* bad thing about you, but try to remember all the good things people have said about you this last week. I'll bet the compliments outnumber the insults 100 to 1!"

"Everyone has to endure setbacks, sweetheart! But I know you'll get through it and come out ahead, like you always do!"

So, men, what's the problem with these examples? Well, on the surface, these responses appear affirming and optimistic. You listen, reflect understanding, show empathy, and reframe the story in a more positive light. All good, right? Actually, only three of those four steps hit the mark. While going three for four in baseball is incredible—a batting average of .750, no less—the reality is most women don't collect statistics. It's not so much what you do over time that counts in the game of communication and human emotion; sometimes, it's all about what you accomplished your most recent time at the plate. From her perspective, your game went like this:

- First at-bat: You listened—hit number one
- Second at-bat: You reflected understanding—hit number two
- Third at-bat: You showed empathy—hit number three
- Fourth at-bat: You tried to fix her *emotionally*—big "whiff!"

Just like that, you struck out on your last try, when another hit could have driven in the winning run.

Remember, it comes down to her premise for communicating! Is she *really* asking for help or simply looking for validation? If it's help she wants, she'll probably ask for it. If it's validation she needs, the last thing she wants you to do is marginalize her misery. Don't reframe her story in a more positive light or attempt to lift her from the emotional state that propelled her to come to you in the first place. What's wrong with trying to cheer her up, you wonder? *Timing.* This may come as a shock to the male mind, but a woman doesn't always *want* to feel better—not until she's good and ready. What she really desires in these moments is a companion to commiserate with, not a knight in shining armor. Asking her to see things through rose-colored glasses not only fails to work, it can actually make things worse. With that in mind, let's revisit the previous examples and look at more effective responses:

WHIFF: "Honey, that's really rough, but you shouldn't let it affect you. You're better than those people."

HIT: "Honey, that's really rough—I don't know why people do those kinds of things."

WHIFF: "Sure one person said *one* bad thing about you, but try to remember all the good things people have said about you this last week. I'll bet the compliments outnumber the insults 100 to 1!"

HIT: "It's never fun when people say bad things about you. I'm sorry that happened."

WHIFF: "Everyone has to endure setbacks, sweetheart! But I know you'll get through it and come out ahead, like you always do!"

HIT: "Wow . . . just when things were going so right this happens! It's got to be frustrating."

Can you sense the difference? Forget the emotional rescue. Don't try to pull her from the pit of woe. Instead, jump in with her and stay a while. Just listen, reflect, empathize and let go of the rest. As much as women generally want their men to talk more, in this case less really is more. Now what man can't get behind *that*?

FOOD FOR THOUGHT: What some men see as female "nagging" is a form of communication that's actually good for them, according to the book, *The Case for Marriage* (Linda J. Waite and Maggie Gallagher, Broadway Books, 2001). It turns out that encouraging men to watch their speed while driving; cut back on smoking, drinking, and TV watching; keep medical appointments; eat more nutritious foods; and establish better sleep habits really pays off in the form of longer, healthier lives.

... WHAT A GUY NEEDS

Don't worry, men, it's your turn to get some attention. Yes, ladies, as little as men seem to need in the way of communication calories, they do gripe about how those calories are served. This is especially true when you ask a favor or make a request. Approach men and requests as you would if you were introducing solid food back into the diet of a child recovering from the flu. You wouldn't think about spicy appetizers, gourmet recipes or fine china. No, you would likely serve the blandest food in your kitchen on your most simple plate. In short, you would have only two goals: Put food in child's stomach; keep food in child's stomach.

This is how men want you to serve things up: Just say it to them plain and simple—in a way they can digest. Sure, there are plenty of television dramas that feature men who engage effortlessly in witty conversation and double entendres with their scripted lovers, but most "real-world" men don't operate that way. Singer Billy Joel summed it up for most guys when he said, "I don't want clever conversation . . . I never want to work that hard." True, your man might be a hard worker in many other ways, but chances are he doesn't enjoy laboring overtime to find your point. If it's too hard to find—if the meat of your request is obscured like Waldo in a sea of extraneous details—he might hear only chatter and miss the request entirely.

Put another way, a woman's way of communicating a request to a man is often like those vultures on a nature show, circling their dying prey far below. They go around and around—and *around again*. They know full-well what they're after. Still, they just don't have it in them go down there and take what they want. Instead, they bide their time ever so cautiously until they're absolutely certain that it's safe to land. In similar fashion, a woman's words sometimes circle and circle around a man's ear but fail to arrive at the mark. While she may feel confident that her point is quite clear, all he hears are words and sentences. Take a look at the dialogue below and you can see the vultures circling:

MIKE: We've had a pretty nice drive so far, don't you think?

[Ambient sound of road noise cut by the shriek of a wiper blade on a dry windshield]

CAROL: Yes, it's been really enjoyable. It's nice to get out for a while and drive.

[Short pause; ambient sound of road noise interrupted again by wiper blade; Carol jerks slightly]

MIKE: Yep, sure is . . .

CAROL: The weather hasn't been at all what I thought. We really lucked out. It only rained there for a half an hour or so.

[Wiper blade . . .]

MIKE: Yeah, the forecast had it wrong after all. I try not to pay too much attention to what they say about the weather.

CAROL: Well, by the looks of it, they really did get it wrong. You know I'm seeing a lot of blue sky already. Just a few dark puffy clouds left. I think it's clearing up, babe!

[Mike leans forward, looks up through windshield, shakes head with satisfaction]

MIKE: You know, I think you're right! I think . . . . *[Wiper blade]* . . . we're going to have sun for the rest of our trip!

Sound familiar? Let's make sense of what *really* happened here in the simplest terms. First let's get inside Carol's head . . .

- What Carol *really* wants: *For the infernal screeching of the wiper blade to stop!*
- How Carol appears on the outside: *hopeful, happy, content*
- How Carol is *really* feeling: *Annoyed, frustrated, unheard*
- What Carol attempted to say: *Please turn off the windshield wipers, Mike.*
- What Carol actually said: *I love long drives in good weather, Mike.*

Now let's have a look at things from Mike's point of view . . .

- What Mike heard Carol say: *I love long drives in good weather, Mike.*
- What Mike thinks Carol was attempting to say: *I love long drives in good weather, Mike.*
- How Mike thinks Carol is *really* feeling: *Hopeful, happy, content*
- What Mike thinks Carol *really* wants: *To chit-chat during their long drive.*

Can you see how Carol's "circling" got her nowhere with Mike? He was as oblivious to the request as he was to the screeching wiper blade! Many men are wired exactly the same way.

But not all men are like Mike. Some actually do get the sense that something's being asked of them, as elusive as that *something* might be. Still, there's no guarantee that they'll have the patience or decoding wherewithal to solve your riddle. This is where so many women go wrong—those moments when they think, "I don't get it. He should just know what I need!" Actually, that's what you have girlfriends and sisters for! They do get it because it's in their communication wiring. Go ahead and lean on your female inner circle to satisfy some of those unmet communication needs. Your man will probably never become a clairvoyant, nor will he ever learn to effectively talk in code. He is hard-wired male, which makes him both insufferable and irresistibly attractive at the same time.

Embrace your fundamental communication differences and learn to say what you want. It's really not that hard. It just takes practice—practice thinking it through and practice phrasing it. Let's return to our "windshield wiper" scenario and demonstrate the kind of internal dialogue Carol might have to help her form a request that is polite, concise, and unmistakably transparent:

1. What do I want? *Well, I'd really like Mike to turn off the wipers. They're annoying.*
2. How should I go about getting what I want? *Well, I haven't had much luck dropping hints. It really only works if I come right out and ask.*
3. How should I phrase my request? *How about, "Hey honey, those wipers are so annoying!" Hmmm, no, that sounds like complaining . . . like I'm blaming him for not doing something about it earlier. How about, "Hey honey, could you turn off the wipers?" Yes, that's good. It's short, sweet, and to the point.*

And with that, Carol is thinking clearly and acting decisively, exactly how Mike likes it! She asks, he responds; she's happy, he's happy.

CHAPTER 3

Individual Appetites for Communication

Now that we've recognized some broad gender differences, we turn our attention next to what romantic partners can do to satisfy one another's appetites for communication as *individuals*. Male or female, we all come into romantic partnerships with very unique perspectives, experiences, and emotional triggers. The older and more experienced we are, the more layers there are to peel away to get to the root of why we think, feel, and react the way we do. Truly learning your partner as an individual is certainly an ambitious endeavor. Still, it can be extremely rewarding if you apply the requisite patience and determination. Once you get to know someone's deepest communication needs and they become intimately familiar with yours, your relationship has the chance to become a bedrock of comfort and emotional safety—a place that feels like home. Few things in life are better than feeling truly understood.

So, how do you get started on the journey toward communication Nirvana? The short answer is to get an idea of all the types of communication in your arsenal. Does he prefer phone calls or in-person dialogue? Does she enjoy receiving little texts throughout the day? Once you know your partner's preferences, then you can think about frequency, intensity, and duration. You wouldn't care to waste your time wondering how often you should buy chocolates for your partner if, in truth, your partner hates chocolate. So for good measure, we'll list several modes of communication to help you identify your preferences, separating them into two general categories: spoken and written. Of course, we won't be able to think of everything, but this will be a good start.

Spoken Communication
1. Face-to-face: Planned (dates or scheduled one-on-one time)
2. Face-to-face: Spontaneous ("pillow talk" before bed; random *I love yous*)
3. Skype or FaceTime® (video conferencing when you're apart)
4. Live phone calls (check-ins from work; calls from the road before bed)
5. Phone messages (random reminders that you're thinking about her/him)
6. Radio dedications (OK—this is a stretch, but more power to you)

FOOD FOR THOUGHT: The average length of a phone call in 1987 was 2.33 minutes. In 2012 it dropped to 1.8 minutes, which suggests that people are choosing more modern forms of electronic communication (statista.com)

Written Communication
1. Old-fashioned letters (if you're 30 or younger, just skip to the next item)
2. Emails (for times when you want to spell out your feelings more carefully)
3. Hand-written notes (random love messages left on car windshields or a nightstand)
4. Greeting cards (the "just because" kind, in particular)
5. Texting/messaging (by far the most popular form of keeping in touch)
6. Smoke signals, sky writing, messages on the beach (whatever floats your boat)

FOOD FOR THOUGHT: Even though Americans in their 20s and 30s text message most (usage is 1,130 sent/1,110 received per month), middle-aged Americans are catching on (usage for 35-44 year olds is 726 sent/831 received per month; usage for 45-54 year olds is 473 sent/525 received per month). (Alex Cocotas, *Business Insider*, March 22, 2013).

With these two lists in front of you, you can identify your specific preferences. In reading through them, you probably noticed some forms of communicating you do all the time, a couple of types you haven't really thought of using, and others that you wish you would receive more often. Once you're in touch with your own likes and dislikes, you can start synching with your partner's preferences. Make no mistake: It's a process that takes some attention, care, and fine-tuning.

Just ask Don. He could tell you how much effort he made to improve the communication in his relationship. But then again, he wouldn't be able to do so without flashing a huge smile. Don is a pretty simple guy. He has never been the life-of-the-party type, nor does he particularly enjoy long, drawn-out conversations—unless, of course, they involve subjects that he is truly passionate about. As it turns out, one of the things he is truly passionate about is his wife, Cynthia. Still, he doesn't easily express that passion through an abundance of words, a fact that used to make Don feel he wasn't measuring up. On that point, Don's suspicions were partially correct. Cynthia was much more talkative than Don. More importantly, she relied quite a bit on verbal communication to feel emotionally connected. Don, on the other hand, was just as likely to feel connected sitting quietly next to her on the couch watching a football game.

Don felt stretched in this area. He knew the communication "what," namely that Cynthia liked face-to-face talking. He also had a pretty good idea of her love-metabolic needs, particularly the "how often" variable.

While she wasn't particularly fond of heavy discussions, per say, or talking for long periods of time, she truly seemed to enjoy light and cheerful conversation, a reality that would have been fine with Don if it weren't for the fact that she liked *so much of it*! In spite of all he knew about his wife, he still struggled to keep pace with the need. And as much as Cynthia understood and appreciated Don, she also knew that she was craving more communication.

But that was then. Determined to make things better, Don rolled up his sleeves and started the tedious, yet rewarding, work of exploration. He asked her questions, did some thinking, and started experimenting. In doing so, Don discovered that there were ways other than face-to-face chats to satisfy his wife's hunger for words. In particular, Don struck communication gold when he learned that Cynthia adored hand-written notes almost as much as she loved to gab. In fact, after a few trial runs, he found that one well-timed, creatively delivered note inspired more intimate feelings than a handful of conversations ever did. This was a huge discovery for Don. It even surprised Cynthia!

Sometimes, he would simply leave a note on the refrigerator, such as, "Have a great day. I'll be thinking about you." Other times he would get more adventurous, scratching out a simple, four-line poem and placing it carefully in the medicine cabinet so it fell to the countertop when she opened it first thing in the morning. Slowly but surely, he learned how to adjust the frequency, duration, and intensity until he found the right mix for Cynthia. Over time, he discovered that he could satisfy her appetite best by writing notes a couple times a month (frequency), keeping the content fairly light and succinct (duration), and finding creative ways to deliver them (intensity).

It took some time to find the solution to this subtle yet confounding love-metabolic gap, but Don and Cynthia worked it out and are far better for it. Sure, they still have plenty to work on, but Don now feels so much relief from knowing that he is able to express his love for his wife in a way that she is truly able to receive. He doesn't feel so much pressure now to be someone he's not. Cynthia has learned a thing or two, as well. She has come to understand that her appetite for communication is not satisfied by the spoken word alone. Sure, she still longs for more conversation, but she can't deny how much more connected and emotionally safe she feels with Don since he started his note-writing campaign.

We could offer a hundred other examples of couples who have figured things out. What they all have in common, though, is that they actually *communicated* about communication. Over time, chat after chat, they uncovered what was needed. Then they determined the right recipe to satisfy the hunger by asking lots of questions: Should I call? If so, how many times a day? Just a check-in or an in-depth discussion? What about texts? Do texts actually mean as much as a call? If so, how many texts a day is my partner expecting? How important is it to add a "smiley face" or "heart"?

And the questions, as inane as they may seem, go on and on. Still, they are questions you really need to ask if you're serious about *learning the burn*. Once you truly understand and know how to meet your romantic partner's metabolic needs for communication, you are well on your way to a place of deeper understanding, security and love.

Couple's Quiz: **COMMUNICATION**

This is the first "couple's quiz" of many to come throughout the book. Answer each question by rating the variable of F.I.D. using a number from the scale below. Then ask your partner to do the same. You'll add the total scores to a worksheet in the concluding chapter.

How satisfied are you with the **COMMUNICATION** in your relationship?

SUBJECT	FREQUENCY	INTENSITY	DURATION	SCORE
Sample	4	0	1	5

For you . . .

SUBJECT	FREQUENCY	INTENSITY	DURATION	SCORE
Communication				

For your partner . . .

SUBJECT	FREQUENCY	INTENSITY	DURATION	SCORE
Communication				

Rating Scale
5 = very satisfied; **4** = satisfied; **3** = somewhat satisfied;
2 = somewhat dissatisfied; **1** = dissatisfied; **0** = completely dissatisfied

Total Score Key
0–5 = Needs a lot of work; **6–10** = Needs some attention; **11–15** = Doing well

CHAPTER 4

Communication Made Queasy

There is a flip-side to love metabolism. Sometimes it isn't a matter of filling a need; sometimes it's all about what a person *doesn't need*. In other words, you not only have to learn how to satisfy your partner's hunger, you also have to figure out what they *can't stomach*. This is especially true with communication. For example, you can feed your partner poetic, hand-written notes to their heart's delight. But then if you elicit nausea with a few inadvertent put-downs in front of friends, you won't get very far in creating deeper understanding, security and love. In this chapter, we'll explore some common communication habits that can be very difficult for many people to digest.

What is palatable and digestible versus what is unsavory and "purgible" is entirely subjective. People have various thresholds, formed from personality variables and external factors, such as family culture and interpersonal experiences. Thus, their tolerance for lower forms of communication can vary dramatically. For instance, one person's idea of an emotionally healthy Thanksgiving experience might feature a quiet dinner, selective conversation, and formal expressions of gratitude; another person's idea of normality might be a fast and furious feast, lots of interrupting and loud laughter, and hours of heated political debate. To be fair, there is no right way or wrong way to communicate. Sure, there is what is socially or culturally acceptable, in general, but social and cultural norms can shift depending on the context. For example, the norms of a few guys in a high school locker room change once they venture outdoors. What they're comfortable saying to one another in the stench of a poorly ventilated room would likely never be heard in the company of a mixed-gender group of friends in the hallway.

Thus, it's all-important to learn the ins and outs of your own "culture" as a couple. What words belong on the "forbidden" list? What kinds of unsavory communication make her stomach turn? What low-brow expressions tend to make him feel like he's under attack? Naturally, you have to spend quite a bit of time with someone to learn all this. Don't be intimidated, though. It's not rocket science! Chances are your romantic partner's least favorite forms of communication fall into one of the following categories:

1. Sarcasm
2. Criticism
3. Teasing
4. Debate
5. Disengagement (not communicating)

SARCASM

You have to be careful with this one! There are many types and degrees of sarcasm. On one extreme, there are light, playful, tongue-in-cheek expressions. Consider this one that a woman affectionately serves up to another couple after church (as her husband chuckles): "The day Ed stays awake through an entire sermon is the day I expect to see an ice skating rink open in hell." On the other extreme is the dark side of sarcasm, which is deeply personal and cutting. Imagine the scenario above, except now the wife is sporting a scowl and her husband is staring at the floor: "Well, you know Ed: He's not interested enough to stay awake during anything important, like church . . . the kids' recital . . . his brother's wedding . . . but football, now that's a *different story*." Yes, this second one has razor blades attached to it. It's never a good idea to go to such toxic depths with your sarcasm, no matter how tough you think your target is. With any communication, there is a point at which human decency should prevail, and that line can only be established through an intimate understanding of your partner's stomach for sarcasm. Look, sarcasm isn't bad, in itself. In reality, it's just a bunch of words thrown together in sentences. Sarcasm, like any kind of "dig", is only as damaging as the people giving and receiving make it out to be. Your job, then, is two-fold: 1. Monitor your own feelings and intentions as the giver, and 2. Seek to truly understand how sarcasm, in all its forms, affects your recipient. Remember, that recipient is also the one whose heart you should protect at all costs.

Let's assume, though, that you're one of those couples that revels in sarcasm. If that's the case, it's safe to assume that there is a good deal of trust and understanding in your relationship and that you both probably have fairly thick skin. Perhaps you grew up in a household where sarcasm was not only tolerated, it was championed. Maybe it was regarded as an integral part of your family's communication culture, a type of playful, competitive demonstration of intelligent wit that invoked laughter and good feelings. More power to you if you're paired with someone who feels the same way about sarcasm.

Chances are, though, you are paired with someone who isn't exactly like you when it comes to communication preferences. If your partner grew up in one of those "if you can't say nothin' nice, don't say nothin' at all" households, you could be in for some rough weather and hurt feelings. It may be challenging, but you'll have to hold back and self-censor. Pay close attention to your partner's reactions and be thoughtful enough to ask if your sarcasm is offensive. If it is, freely apologize and ask for help in understanding what, in particular, is offensive. Now, we're not suggesting you need to completely rewire your personality to accommodate another. If your partner is easily offended, might that be a sign that you're better suited to someone who has thicker skin? Maybe. But if your sense of self is based largely on sarcastic wit, then it's probably safe to say that your self-concept could be built on firmer ground.

Love is all about building up your romantic partner and making him or her feel safe enough to reciprocate that love. If your sarcastic tendencies tear at the fabric of that confidence, is it really worth the damage? Is it that difficult to choose a more straight-forward way to say things, in the first place? It really just comes down to which you value more: a communication style or the person you supposedly love. Remember, too, that the heart you wound through careless communication is also the place you look to for love and validation. A wounded heart can only give so much back.

CRITICISM

As with sarcasm, criticism can be extremely damaging. Again, this entirely depends on your partner's internal constitution and upbringing. Some people see criticism as a great motivator for accomplishment, a catalyst for personal growth. Others take criticism as a sign of disapproval and rejection. Another thing to consider is whether criticism is given privately or publicly. For some, criticism is tolerable within the confines of their own homes. In mixed company, however, they find any slight from their trusted companion unacceptable and embarrassing.

To be sure, a little bit of constructive criticism is good for anyone, and we all should learn to embrace it. Still, you need to see criticism on a continuum, just as you do sarcasm. At one extreme is the kind of cancerous criticism that does anything but inspire personal growth. Instead, it tears down confidence, instills doubt, and destroys trust—especially when it comes from the one we are supposed to trust with our hearts.

FOOD FOR THOUGHT: Dr. John Gottman advises you to take your partner's side! When you find yourselves in a discussion in which your partner is under fire in some way, don't side with the opposition or find fault in front of others. Instead, be publicly supportive. Even if you believe your partner is in the wrong or is being unreasonable, don't openly disagree. Wait until there is a more appropriate, private time to share your feelings with your partner. (*The Seven Principles for Making Marriage Work*, Harmony Books, 1999).

Know your partner. Know how he grew up. Was he an only child who thrived on high-performance and praise, with parents who used only encouraging words to both commend and correct? Did he grow up with a lot of pressure from highly demanding, perfectionist parents? Remember, romantic partners don't only hear *you* when you criticize; they unconsciously hear the voices of past caregivers, too. People who have endured a lot of debilitating criticism, and those who have endured almost none, can both react strongly to perceived criticism. Most people fall somewhere in the middle, of course.

Whatever their upbringing, the real question is people's resiliency. To what degree did they assimilate all those parental messages? How do they, as individuals, perceive various forms of criticism and how do they let it affect their self-esteem now? What is their threshold for absorbing criticism? When does it become personal? At what point does it take a turn toward the destructive? It's really worth finding out. At the same time you're learning all this, take a good look at your own motives and intentions. Before you think about leveling any kind of criticism, apply a critical eye to what's going on inside *you*. What is it that you're trying to accomplish? Is your criticism designed to create a healthy change in your relationship or is it a power-play designed to make yourself feel better by tearing your partner down?

With patience and work, you can answer all these questions and start to make healthy changes. Think back to previous instances when you told your lover that you were displeased with something. How did he or she react? Think about your approach. Could you have reworded the criticism or not pointed fingers? Could you have found a way to make the target of your criticism the *thing* that irritates you rather than the *person* doing it? Working through past altercations can help you discover the best ways to ask for change in the future. What you can't figure out from memory you can discover by simply asking your romantic partner. Don't hesitate. Be emotionally courageous and demonstrate trust by requesting feedback, right there in the moment of criticism or shortly afterwards. Doing so can be stressful, but it can also build the kind of trust and gratitude that only moments of honesty can bring.

FOOD FOR THOUGHT: In "The Ideal Praise to Criticism Ratio," (an article in the *Harvard Business Review*, March 15, 2013), Emily Heaphy revealed that it may take six positive comments to override the bad feelings caused by one negative comment.

TEASING

Teasing is the playful cousin to criticism and sarcasm. And yes—teasing lies somewhere on a continuum, as well. On the positive side are those humorous exchanges that signal a kind of fraternal affection. On the dark side are the kind of debilitating attacks routinely administered by the local school-yard bully. As with sarcasm and criticism, much of our ability to receive teasing of any kind depends on our family culture and experiences. (If you grew up in a house full of brothers, you're probably an expert in both dishing it out *and* receiving it). As the ways that teasing can affect relationships are so similar to what we've already described, we won't belabor the point. It's important to become intimately aware of your partner's ability to handle teasing, both through exploring his or her childhood experiences and working as a couple to determine the line that separates playful banter from destructive dialogue.

DEBATE

Lest some of you who enjoy intense religious or political discussions take offense, let's define what we mean by "debate." What we are talking about here is not so much arguing different beliefs, positions or opinions. True, such exchanges can become heated and even damaging to a relationship if they're not approached with tact and empathy. On the flip side, *respectful* debate can actually enrich a relationship. It can be the catalyst for meaningful personal change, as couples challenge one another to consider new ideas and discard irrational beliefs and assumptions.

This is not the kind of "debate" we're considering. What we have in mind are tedious, nit-picky exchanges between romantic partners that delay, disrupt and, in some cases, derail conversations. Imagine one person attempting to tell a story while the other incessantly challenges the facts and makes corrections. Now you have our version of "unhealthy debating." Couples can get sucked into this kind of fruitless dialogue so easily. True, some really don't mind it. Others don't realize they're doing it. Still others see it as an exhausting exercise in futility, zapping all the fun out of story-telling. In the worst cases, this communication pattern becomes so pervasive that one partner becomes reluctant to share stories at all, especially in the company of others.

To illustrate, we give you Mark and Sue, who are attempting to enjoy an evening out with another couple:

SUE: So . . . Mark and I had the funniest thing happen the other day. We were heading out of the city during a wind storm last Thursday, and it took something like 30 minutes just to go a few blocks.

MARK [*interrupts*]: Actually, Sue, if you'll remember the storm started up Thursday evening but it was Friday that we were trying to get out of town.

SUE: Oh . . . OK. That's right. Anyway, on Friday we were driving through the city and it took forever because every traffic light was out on the way.

MARK: Yeah, it was pretty bad, but that's not what took us so long. The truth is some of the lights were out, but it was all the debris on the road that stopped traffic so badly.

SUE: Yes, that, too. But I swear we were stuck for 20 minutes at one intersection because no one was there to direct traffic.

MARK: Yes there was! There was a cop there, don't you remember? Even with him there it took a long time, probably more like 10 minutes, though, not 20.

SUE: OK, right, but I know it took 20 minutes either way. Remember, I looked at the time and told you I was worried because I wanted to get out of the traffic before dark and that we only had about a half hour until sunset? Well, we just made it before sunset.

MARK: We made it out a good 15 minutes before sunset, but whatever . . . it's fine. Go ahead.

SUE: [*deep breath*] Anyway . . . . we were stuck there for *a while*. I was getting pretty nervous about the lightning and thunder mostly, but I definitely wanted to get out of the traffic before dark.

MARK [*laughing*]: Lightning? All you kept talking about was how you've been scared of strong wind since you were little girl. Remember we talked about that hurricane you lived through? I had to remind you that we don't live in Florida.

SUE *[sarcastically]*: OK . . . *whatever*, Mark. Yeah, I guess I'm scared of many things. Good thing I have *you* there to keep me calm.

MARK: Well, I'm just saying . . .

SUE *[eyes rolling]*: How about not saying anything? Try that one for a while . . .

Have you ever been *that* couple—the one sitting opposite a couple like Mark and Sue? How awkward are *those* occasions? While the tension is obvious to you and everyone else in the group, they keep stepping deeper into the conversational quagmire, oblivious to the way their behavior is beginning to stink up the evening. It's like they can't help themselves; they just get sucked into the drama. Like Mark, some play the part of the detail junky—the instigator who just can't leave well enough alone. Others, like Sue, play the part of the enabler turned co-conspirator. Though resistant at first to the incessant peppering, they eventually get lured in and join the unconscious campaign to ruin yet another group date.

For some people, this kind of conversational sabotage is insufferable. It's tedious, stifling, and at times, a complete emotional drain! They just want to get through their story, however trivial it may be. They don't sweat the details because the details don't really matter. They don't want to be edited. *Does anyone*, for that matter? Sue certainly didn't enjoy it. She was never able to get to her point during dinner. By the end, all that was left was eye-rolling and interpersonal tension thick enough to box up and take home. Whatever her intended effect, it was completely undone by annoying debate.

Mark represents the other side of the equation. He's a natural at debating details. Now, on the surface, he may seem the type of guy who enjoys stirring the pot. Going a step further, you might even think that he's deliberately trying to sabotage Sue's story. That's not true. Mark is like many men out there for whom the tireless quest for accuracy is almost as instinctual as breathing. It's anything but deliberate. In reading the dialogue above, you may have noticed that Mark didn't seem particularly agitated. In fact, he wasn't. It was simply business-as-usual. His mind went so swiftly to fact-checking land, he hardly had time for self-awareness.

Let's suppose the tables were turned. What if Mark got a taste of his own medicine and *his* story were hijacked in similar fashion? How would he like it, *then*? Well, this may come as a surprise, but Mark might like it just fine. As we said, it's natural. In dialogue with his buddies over sports statistics, engineering specs, or whatever, he routinely has his own facts challenged and he gladly takes the bait every time. Tangents don't detract from the story if it means getting the facts straight. Indeed, for left-brain-leaning men like Mark, nothing kills a good story like an erroneous fact.

Suffice it to say, Sue and Mark have much different love-metabolic tolerance for "debate." Mark consumes it effortlessly, as if it were on the list of major food groups; she gets just a little and begins to feel sick to her stomach. So what can they do about it? For Mark, it all starts with self-awareness. He won't get out of the gates, however, without Sue's help. She should find an appropriate time—away from the heat of the moment—when she can calmly express her feelings to Mark. She needs to understand that her sarcastic replies and eye-rolling offer Mark only a fleeting glimpse into the true depths of her frustrations and do very little to affect lasting, positive change. Once she's successful in reaching Mark and he begins to understand what "debate" is doing to their relationship, he can start rewiring his brain. Impossible? Not at all! Armed with understanding and the will to change, he only has a few more tasks to complete:

1. Talk with Sue and revisit past conversations that went awry.
2. Identify specific moments in those conversations when things took a turn for the worse, considering what he might have said differently (we call it a "redo" in therapy).
3. Begin to recognize which kinds of corrections annoy her and which, if any, are welcomed (e.g., a fact that is crucial to the integrity of the story).
4. The next time Sue shares a story, think about her purpose in telling it, let go of the need to correct her, and reflect on how debating has caused harm in the past.
5. Practice, practice and practice some more!

Mark will no doubt put his foot in his mouth more than a few times on his way to self-mastery, but eventually he'll get comfortable with the new communication approach. He needs to be patient and stay the course, as does Sue.

DISENGAGEMENT

Sometimes it's what you don't say that hurts the most. As much as sarcasm, criticism, teasing, and debating can damage a relationship, it's the ultimate form of lower communication—disengagement—that's the most lethal. Commonly called "the silent treatment," it occurs when one partner or the other withdraws words, attention, and care. Sometimes disengagement is the result of an unconscious attempt to escape the tension and pressure of relational conflict. Other times, it's a conscious form of punishment. Either way, it's the most tangible sign that a relationship is in serious danger of dissolution. Relationship guru Dr. John Gottman of the University of Washington calls it "moving away." The irony is thick! You would think that the fighting, bickering, and arguing—all part of what Gottman terms, "moving against"—is what tears couples apart, but the cold silence of withdrawal is the real killer.

That said, some people can stomach disengagement better than others. In fact, a small degree of disengagement can be quite beneficial, at least for a short period of time. We frequently suggest that couples develop "safety plans" to help them cool down before they say and do things they will soon regret. These plans often involve a reasonable amount of time away from one another to gather thoughts and composure. Couples may take five minutes or a few hours. It may even take a very strategic "therapeutic separation" lasting days or weeks. The difference with this kind of withdrawal is just that—it's therapeutic. It's planned, it's carried out in an emotionally safe way, and each partner knows what to expect. Once break time is over, a couple "re-engages" one another to work through the issue. The problem with "unplanned" disengagement is that it's not emotionally safe! Its damaging effects are stealthy, gradual and eventually suffocating. It may start out as a stubborn stand-off, but it can gradually suck the life out of your relationship. Sooner or later, you may start to feel very alone and very abandoned, depending on your tolerance level for disengagement.

Disengagement is very similar to the word, "detachment." Detaching from the one you love is precarious business because as Dr. Sue Johnson points out in her book, *Hold Me Tight*, relationships are all about the quality of attachments. In short, we all have an innate need to emotionally attach to other human beings. It's primal and kicks in the minute we're born. Even so, many of us have learned that we can't always trust caregivers, friends, and romantic partners. For some, it takes an awful lot of trust to let down their guard and let love happen. It's not hard to imagine, then, how unsettling it could be when the one you trust with your heart begins to withdraw their love and attention. How much these episodes of "detachment" affect you depends on how safely connected you feel, on your past experiences, and on deeply ingrained personality factors that determine your resiliency.

Take Paul, for example, a 31-year-old man who has been committed to Jean for three years. In that time, he has formed a real bond with Jean. Still, for reasons he doesn't understand, she is beginning to withdraw. What Paul doesn't know is that Jean is upset over how much time he spends reading alone at night before bed. She sometimes feels lonely, neglected, and even abandoned, depending on the night. Instead of engaging Paul to express how she feels, she has chosen to go cold. When Paul asked her about it, she stonewalled him with denials and deflections. All he knows is that she's quieter, less responsive, and has stopped initiating conversation altogether. She is reluctant to make eye contact. In fact, all their communication—talking, emailing, texting—is nothing more than a trickle.

While all this is perplexing and disheartening for Paul, the truth is he's built to handle it quite well. Let's take a look at Paul's profile:

Paul
- Born to stable, loving parents
- Only child
- Enjoyed a comparatively safe and secure childhood environment
- Regular communication with parents; visits at least four times a year
- Had only a couple close friends growing up; an introvert, mostly
- Very independent spirit; comfortable on his own, doing his own thing
- Works mostly from home and has a couple of time-consuming hobbies
- Had one close romantic relationship through college that lasted three and a half years; broke up amicably—mutual decision
- Opened up like never before with Jean; very attached
- Feels like this is the first time he's really been in love with someone; even considering marriage

Let's make sense of the profile. From Paul's earliest days—even from his first year of life—he got the sense that the world, in general, was a pretty safe place to be. When he cried, he was heard. When he needed warmth and comfort, he was held. The caregivers that acted as the "north star" in Paul's life constellation remained fixed and reliable. To this day, they are an emotional anchor and a source of unconditional support. Thus, Paul has learned a valuable emotional lesson, namely that some people in this world are *safe*. Paul has been spared the destabilizing attachment anxiety that befalls so many who were not lucky enough to have dependable caregivers. In other words, people and relationships are not so scary to Paul.

This fact was only reinforced by his one, long-term relationship with a girl during college. They truly enjoyed their time together, and even when they both came to realize that they were moving in different directions in life, they broke up very deliberately and peaceably. Thus, Paul's attachment trust remained intact. And even now when his trust is on trial due to Jean's disengagement, his relationship anxiety doesn't extend beyond the confines of his current relationship. That's a good sign for Paul.

Another thing Paul has going for him is that he finds great solace in being alone with his own thoughts and ideas. He has a couple of hobbies that he can pursue completely on his own. The truth is, he's always preferred to either stay home with Jean, read, or work on his projects rather than go out on the town with all the crowds and noise. This is a good thing, given his situation. As unnerving and foreign as her disengagement has been, he has found sanctuary in retreating to his books and hobbies. In short, he knows how to occupy himself with healthy distractions.

But in spite of his personality and coping abilities, Paul has never felt more off-balance. This is because he has never been so attached—so *emotionally connected*—to another person. Paul has learned the painful truth that along with the great rewards of intimate attachment come the inevitable risks of grief and loss should that connection break. Paul loves

Jean. He has come to rely on her more than anyone. He wants to marry her and spend the rest of his life in her company. All this is true, but it's also true that she has never been more emotionally *unreliable*, a fact that has knocked his world out of orbit.

So as difficult as this is for Paul, his chances of successfully coping with Jean's disengagement are pretty good. Let's now take a look at Jean's profile.

Jean
- Born to loving but very flawed parents
- Father left when she was five years old; had short-lived, occasional contact thereafter
- Mother became over-involved and smothering; sometimes acted the part of controlling parent, other times of best friend
- Had several boyfriends as a teenager and during her early twenties
- Lots of relationship volatility with dramatic break-ups
- One long-term relationship in her late twenties that went off and on for four years; lived together; partner eventually got frustrated and left
- More inclined to be out and about, surrounded by lots of social energy
- Anxiously attached to Paul; never loved anyone more, including members of her own family
- Feels like she might want to get married, but starts to feel sick to her stomach when her mind goes there

And the list goes on. She is what we would call "anxiously attached," not just to Paul, but to practically everyone she has ever been involved with. The simple fact is that a lifetime of volatile, erratic, and unreliable relationships has Jean scared speechless. She is frightened to the core by how much she loves Paul. When she thinks about marriage, her glimpses of happiness are quickly swallowed up in fear. That's why she is unconsciously disengaging. Misconstruing Paul's nighttime reading habits as a sign of impending doom, she is executing a type of "preemptive strike," an instinctual move to insure that she abandons Paul before he abandons *her*.

It comes down to emotional survival. People like Paul are in a much better position to weather the storm because they've learned to trust people. People like Jean, unfortunately, haven't. It's paramount to really dive in and get to know where your partner falls on the spectrum of attachment resiliency. Get to know his upbringing and his relationship history. Learn what he has learned *about people*. Are they safe? Can they or should they be trusted? If his personality and history line up with Jane's, you can expect some push and pull as you draw close to him.

That doesn't mean you can't form a safe bond with your partner. Attachment challenges are anything but insurmountable. You can get through them if you take the time to learn the various ways attachment anxiety gets triggered. Certainly, don't ever do your own version of disengaging. Chances are it's among your partner's top triggers. Just avoid that defense tactic altogether. It's far better to develop your own "safety plan" if you truly need time away or space to breathe.

Perhaps what you really need isn't time or space, after all, but rather more productive, peaceful ways to express your disappointments, unmet needs, and frustrations. Most relationships do far better with much more directive approaches. Even if the conversation were to become heated, at least you're involved. The conflict would be something you could see, hear, and feel. It might sting, but it's nothing compared to the frostbite you'll get from disengagement! Healthy couples learn to *engage* one another. Sure, they disagree, quarrel, and even yell on occasion, but they don't disengage.

Couple's Quiz: COMMUNICATION MADE QUEASY

Answer each question by rating the variables of F.I.D. using a number from the scale below. Then ask your partner to do the same. Later, you'll add the total scores to a worksheet in the concluding chapter.

How much of a problem is your partner's
use of **SARCASM** toward you?

For you . . .

SUBJECT	FREQUENCY	INTENSITY	DURATION	SCORE
Sarcasm				

For your partner . . .

SUBJECT	FREQUENCY	INTENSITY	DURATION	SCORE
Sarcasm				

Rating Scale
5 = no problem at all; **4** = it's barely a problem; **3** = it's somewhat of a problem;
2 = it's definitely a problem; **1** = it's a considerable problem;
0 = it's a major problem

Total Score Key
0–5 = Needs a lot of work; **6–10** = Needs some attention; **11–15** = Doing well

How much of a problem is your partner's **CRITICISM** of you?

For you . . .

SUBJECT	FREQUENCY	INTENSITY	DURATION	SCORE
Criticism				

For your partner . . .

SUBJECT	FREQUENCY	INTENSITY	DURATION	SCORE
Criticism				

How much of a problem is your partner's **TEASING**?

For you . . .

SUBJECT	FREQUENCY	INTENSITY	DURATION	SCORE
Teasing				

For your partner . . .

SUBJECT	FREQUENCY	INTENSITY	DURATION	SCORE
Teasing				

Rating Scale
5 = no problem at all; **4** = it's barely a problem; **3** = it's somewhat of a problem;
2 = it's definitely a problem; **1** = it's a considerable problem;
0 = it's a major problem

Total Score Key
0–5 = Needs a lot of work; **6–10** = Needs some attention; **11–15** = Doing well

How much of a problem is nit-picky **DEBATE**?

For you . . .

SUBJECT	FREQUENCY	INTENSITY	DURATION	SCORE
Debate				

For your partner . . .

SUBJECT	FREQUENCY	INTENSITY	DURATION	SCORE
Debate				

How much of a problem is **DISENGAGEMENT** in your relationship?

For you . . .

SUBJECT	FREQUENCY	INTENSITY	DURATION	SCORE
Disengage				

For your partner . . .

SUBJECT	FREQUENCY	INTENSITY	DURATION	SCORE
Disengage				

Rating Scale
5 = no problem at all; **4** = it's barely a problem; **3** = it's somewhat of a problem;
2 = it's definitely a problem; **1** = it's a considerable problem;
0 = it's a major problem

Total Score Key
0–5 = Needs a lot of work; **6–10** = Needs some attention; **11–15** = Doing well

CHAPTER 5

Too Much Conflict in the Kitchen

Sara is surprised to run into one of her best friends, Jasmine, while making her way through the grocery store. They engage in some minor chit-chat, but Sara can tell that something is off. Jasmine isn't her usual, cheery self.

"Everything OK?" she asks Jasmine.

"Yeah, I'm fine. Good. Doing great, actually."

Sara raises one eyebrow, tilting her head down incredulously. "Are you sure?"

Jasmine lets out a deep sigh and hangs her head for a moment. "Well, to be honest, Maurice and I have been *fighting* a lot lately and it's wearing me out."

"I'm so sorry to hear that! That doesn't sound good, Jasmine. Not at all."

Later that evening, Sara leaks the secret to her husband, Chuck. To her surprise, he is *not surprised*.

"Yeah, I ran into Maurice yesterday and asked how things were going," says Chuck.

"You're kidding! What did he say?"

"He said everything was going pretty well. When I asked how Jasmine was doing, he kind of shook his head and paused for a second."

"Did he tell you they've been fighting?"

"No, he didn't say that . . . exactly. He said she's been in a bad mood lately, probably because they haven't seen eye to eye on finances. He told me they had had a few heavy discussions about money and that she was taking things way too personally. He mentioned that she stormed off during one of their conversations . . . even accused him of trying to pick a fight with her."

"Hmmm. Jasmine said the same thing."

"Yeah, but that's obviously not how Maurice saw it. He's not sure what he did to make her so upset."

Can you see the love-metabolic mismatch here? Jasmine and Maurice aren't even using the same terminology to describe their recent exchanges. What Jasmine calls a "fight," Maurice calls a "heavy discussion." The dialogue above illustrates two things: 1. two people in a relationship may define "conflict" very differently, and 2. one partner in a relationship may be able to stomach conflict much better than the other.

The fact is, all couples engage in conflict of some kind. Something as trivial as a disagreement over the ideal route to the freeway is arguably somewhere on the spectrum of interpersonal conflict. Most couples struggle much more than that. For some, conflict is almost a daily occurrence. Still, let's not make the mistake of calling all conflict "bad." Without some degree of conflict, and the stress it brings, we would never reach our full potential. Studies have shown that people perform at their best when there is just the right amount of stress in their lives. The same could be said for couples. As comfortable as a relationship that never rocks the boat may seem, you won't sail very far without some good wind and waves. On the other hand, too much wind and waves can capsize the boat and kill you! The key, then, is to find that sweet-spot for relational stress—that place where the level of conflict in your relationship keeps you on your toes but doesn't knock you entirely off balance.

But once again, here is the fundamental problem and the entire premise for our book: Partnerships are made of two individuals with differing love metabolic sensitivities. Whatever *your* healthy threshold for conflict may be, chances are it does not exactly match your partner's. There is much to consider, here; it's not as simple as figuring out where the "one bar" for conflict lies. To really understand the complexity of your romantic partner's stomach for conflict, ask some key questions:

1. When does my partner feel like a discussion becomes a fight?
2. What are the hot-button issues or triggers? What topics are especially volatile?
3. When a disagreement arises, what do I do or say that's upsetting or annoying to my partner?
4. When it comes to arguments, how often is too often (frequency)? What does my partner consider "a lot" of conflict?
5. How much heat can my partner handle before it's too much (intensity)?
6. How long can my partner reasonably hang in there before needing a break (duration)?

By asking questions like these, you can begin the work of decoding the various types and degrees of conflict your partner can digest. At the same time, you can be answering these questions for yourself. In fact, let's go ahead and have you consider how each question applies to you, personally:

1) WHEN DOES A DISCUSSION BECOME A FIGHT?

Of course, your answer entirely depends on your sensitivity to interpersonal tension. How were you raised? Did your family members verbalize their frustrations, raise their voices, or frequently lose their cool? Were they encouraged to confront each other honestly and openly?

Or conversely, was your family one that valued a calm voice and even temperament? Was it one that taught you to keep your frustrations to yourself? Perhaps your family was a little bit of both. In addition to upbringing, much of your tolerance will depend on personality factors. If you enjoy a good debate and have the ability to avoid taking things personally, it might take quite the war of words for you to classify a discussion as a "fight." If, on the other hand, your disposition is one that craves interpersonal peace at all costs, something as slight as a rise in vocal intensity might signal the beginning of battle.

2) WHAT ARE THE HOT-BUTTON ISSUES?

Chances are that not every topic ruffles your feathers. Still, when the subject matter gets a little too personal, it may just unleash your inner beast! For instance, let's suppose you engage in an argument over whether or not the housework you just completed falls into the "job well-done" category. You state your case; he states his. In the end, your work ethic is questioned but your composure remains intact. Later that evening, however, he sarcastically makes the insinuation that "good" mothers don't choose reading magazines over reading to their children. This one makes your blood boil the more you think of it, because it's deeply personal to you. The thought that your partner would call into question your competency as a mother is almost unbearable, and it's just a matter of time until you fire back with sarcasm of your own.

FOOD FOR THOUGHT: Hot-button issues we commonly see in our practices include:

1. Parenting
2. Sex
3. Finances
4. In-laws
5. Friends

So what makes these issues so "hot"? It's the deepest feelings they invoke, which in turn lead to the arguing and fighting. Some people feel:

1. Disrespected
2. Unheard
3. Devalued
4. Unappreciated
5. Overlooked
6. Unworthy
7. Unloved

---

3) WHEN A DISAGREEMENT ARISES, WHAT UPSETS OR ANNOYS YOU?

What tactic does your partner employ that you find irritating or offensive? In her book *Hold Me Tight*, Dr. Sue Johnson mentions several defensive devices that some romantic partners use to combat feelings of vulnerability. One of these is what she terms, "Find the Bad Guy." We call it "The Blame Game," and it's fairly self-explanatory. It's a type of argumentative, one-upping, ping-pong match in which each partner fires back with a comment aimed to prove the other more worthy of scorn. It takes a lot of humility and emotional courage to admit your mistakes, faulty perceptions, and insecurities—to "own your own

*#&^," as mental health professionals affectionately say. It's much easier to point fingers, which effectively diverts attention from your deepest vulnerabilities.

Perhaps it doesn't bother you so much when your partner points the finger at you as much as when you're drawn into what Dr. Johnson calls "The Protest Polka." It's an ugly "dance" that happens when your partner aggressively confronts, makes demands, and criticizes, while you, in turn, retreat and withdraw your attention. It's a brutal cycle for couples. The more your partner hems and haws, the more you withdraw and hide; the more you withdraw and hide, the more your partner desperately engages you.

Another argumentative pitfall occurs when your partner can't let go of the past. Have you ever been haunted by former indiscretions, ones for which you apologized and that you feel were rectified long ago? Still, when the mood strikes and the conflict is sufficiently heated, your partner complicates the issue at hand by piling on extra fuel for the flames. This is not only annoying, but it can also damage trust. It can send the message that problems will not, in fact, ever really be solved and that forgiveness will never truly be earned. Once that seed is planted, confidence in the relationship can only erode from there. How hopeful and motivated to solve problems can you be if the past continually comes back to bite you?

4) WHAT DO YOU CONSIDER "A LOT OF CONFLICT"? HOW MUCH HEAT CAN YOU HANDLE, AND HOW LONG CAN YOU HANG IN THERE?

Again, look at your upbringing and personality. If both have combined to thicken your skin, then it might take a lot of conflict for you to *see it* as "a lot." What's more, many interactions others would find contentious are likely to escape your conflict radar. Thus defining conflict is just as important as counting occurrences. Undaunted by strong feelings and words, you are good at holding your ground for as long as it takes to resolve things. More importantly, you're quickly able to let go of the tension afterwards. If, however, you fall on the sensitive side of the personality spectrum (which is perfectly fine, by the way), your sense of well-being will likely decrease as incidents of perceived conflict increase. You're not so good with intense conflict and all its trappings, including amplified voices, strained facial expressions, and aggressive body language. Even when the tumultuous quaking is over, you're likely to experience a few emotional "aftershocks." Unfortunately, the ill effects of conflict tend to linger with you.

PUTTING IT ALL TOGETHER: KYLE AND KENNA

Below we'll profile Kyle and Kenna, a couple who have different metabolic tolerance levels for conflict. Once you have a chance to get to know Kyle and Kenna individually, we'll present two scenarios, one featuring an escalation of conflict that hurts their relationship, and the other revealing how they compromise to keep the peace.

Kyle's background:
- Father was gentle, kind-hearted, and soft-spoken
- Mother was optimistic and energetic
- One sibling, a brother eight years younger
- Occasional, low-level conflict growing up; tempers rarely ever flared
- Incidents of conflict in the home were usually resolved quickly

Kyle's personality:
- Pleasantly outgoing (like his mother) yet soft-spoken (like his father)
- Tends to keep feelings to himself if annoyed or offended; works it out internally

- Avoids contention if at all possible; negative emotions tend to linger

Kyle's hot-button issue: When he's teased as being the "good boy" who can't break any rules.

Kenna's background:
- Father was fun-loving but also used a lot of foul language and sarcasm when frustrated
- Mother was even-tempered, but very directive; "honest to a fault"
- Several siblings, close in age; mostly sisters; competitive
- Lots of trivial conflict—complaining and blaming; big blow ups once a month or so, usually between sisters, with intense yelling

Kenna's personality:
- Good-natured but feisty; animated
- Quick to point out things that annoy her
- Gets easily worked up but also easily forgives and forgets

Kenna's hot-button issue: Her weight and personal appearance

SCENARIO 1

Kyle arrives home from work late on a Friday evening. He drops his computer bag by the door and scurries back to the bedroom to change clothes, knowing full well he's only got about 15 minutes to get ready. If he takes longer than that, he'll risk making both of them late for Kenna's annual fundraiser. As Kyle arrives, he finds various clothing items strewn around the bed and Kenna frantically brushing and spraying her hair. "Sorry, I'm late, honey," he says with some trepidation, unsure how she'll react. Offering no reply, she peers back at him through the mirror with an expression that says it all: She's not happy. Kyle issues another meager peace offering: "I tried to get out of the office, but my supervisor caught me as I was leaving and asked me to come into his office to go over a report before I left. I felt like I didn't have a choice."

Kenna immediately interjects: "You always have a choice, Kyle. You could have told him straight up that you had to get home right away. I knew this would happen. The problem is you're just too nice." Kyle shrugs his shoulders and flashes a nervous smile.

"Guilty as charged, but what's wrong with that, hon? That's partly why you married me, right?"

"Yes, Kyle, I married you because you're a good guy, but I also get annoyed with you. I just wish you would put your foot down with people sometimes and not be afraid to shake things up once in a while."

A small, pulsing blip now appears on Kyle's conflict radar.

"What do you mean shake things up?"

"You're just always trying too hard to be the good employee. When's the last time you took a sick day? How about *never*? You know, you could have taken some sick time today. Hell, you *should have* taken half the day off to help me get things ready for the event tonight!"

Kyle's blood pressure is now on the rise. He hates it when she gets like this. "So I should be a dishonest employee, then? That's your definition of putting my foot down with people?"

Kenna's reply drips with dark sarcasm. "No, don't be dishonest, Kyle, that would be *horrible!*"

Kyle feels almost knocked over by this sudden wave of tension. He shakes his head, lets out a big breath, and then heads to the closet to pick out his suit for the evening. Kenna goes back to the business of beautification, seemingly un-phased by the exchange. After a couple minutes have passed and Kyle regains his composure, he turns back toward Kenna to check out her dress. Unsure whether she's wearing her outfit for the evening or if she hasn't yet changed from work, Kyle innocently asks, "Is that what you're wearing tonight?" Kenna stops brushing her hair and stares blankly into the mirror. She slowly turns her head, eyes squinting and glazed over.

"Uh, yeah . . . . this is what I'm wearing. What's wrong with it?"

"Nothing . . . nothing at all. It looks great. I was just . . . "

"Just *what*?"

"I just wanted to make sure I'm dressing right for the occasion. You know . . . that we're matching."

Kenna raises her voice. "You don't like what I'm wearing, do you? You don't like how I look in this!"

Kyle tries his best to keep up. "No, I . . . "

Kenna interrupts again. "Sometimes I don't think you like how I look, period! If you wanted a *supermodel*, you should have married one!"

SCENARIO 2

Kyle comes home as described above (we'll skip all the details). After offering his apologies, Kenna replies.

"Well, I would be lying if I didn't tell you I was disappointed."

"I know, honey. I know how important tonight is for you! Again, I'm sorry."

Kenna stops brushing her hair for a moment and looks over at Kyle. "Couldn't you have just told your supervisor that it would have to wait until Monday morning?"

Kyle pauses and purses his lips. "Yeah, I guess I should have. Don't worry. I'll hurry. We'll be on time."

Unsatisfied, Kenna's protest continues. "I mean, I'm glad you're such a hard worker and a reliable employee. You do things the right way. I love that about you. It's just that I would also love it if just once you would break your own rules . . . just tell someone 'no' for a change. That's all."

Kyle tilts his head and raises his eyebrows in momentary thought, then replies with an uncharacteristic devious grin. "Yeah, I suppose one day I should do just *that*—if for no other reason than to see the look on your face when you find out I did."

His awkward attempt at humor catches her off-guard and she laughs, which in turn makes him laugh a little. Changing subjects, Kyle asks, "By the way, is that what you're wearing tonight?"

Kenna freezes for a moment. "Why do you ask?"

"Just wondering what I should wear to the fundraiser. I don't want to under-dress or anything."

"Oh, OK. I thought maybe you didn't like the way I look. Yes, this is what I'm wearing. Do I look good?"

Kyle stops ruffling through his dress shirts and looks directly at Kenna. "You look great, honey. *Really.*"

DISCUSSION

At first glance, there may not seem to be much difference between the two scenarios. Both present a situation involving conflict. Let us say again that conflict in any relationship is inevitable. You might even argue that it's necessary for personal growth, as we mentioned earlier. It may not show on the surface with some couples, but make no mistake, conflict happens no matter what. Sometimes that conflict is swallowed whole before it has a chance to find outward expression. On the other extreme, some couples become so inflamed that they cause a public spectacle with their arguments. Either way, it happens. What's important to realize is that not all conflict is equal in terms of its ability to help or harm a relationship. So again, the two examples you just read may, on the surface, appear to offer only subtle differences. But in reality, each scenario produces vastly different emotional effects: One is toxic to the relationship, while the other actually converts tension into an opportunity to bond.

Given what you know about Kyle and Kenna's backgrounds, you can clearly see why the first scenario is damaging. Both of their hot-buttons are pushed (Dr. Sue Johnson would call them "raw spots"): Accusations of being "too nice" (Kyle) and body image (Kenna). Kenna keeps coming after him with criticism, in spite of Kyle's obvious attempts to deescalate the conflict with apologies and admissions. Even his last-ditch appeal—the feeble reminder that she married him, in part, because he's such a nice guy—withers in the rising heat. The situation ends with fractured feelings, lost respect and diminished trust.

Looking at scenario number one from a F.I.D. perspective (frequency, intensity, and duration), Kenna's onslaught is too intense and too sudden for Kyle. It's like throwing him on the track to run the 100 meter dash without time to properly warm up or stretch. Even then—warmed up or not—Kyle's not much of a runner to begin with. He has to take it slow and is only able to endure short distances. Kenna, on the other hand, has the unique ability to not only run like lightning, but do so over long distances. She's a conflict Olympian, of sorts. Sure, she might come out a little winded at times, but she's always ready for the next race. Meanwhile, Kyle finds himself very winded trying to keep pace with Kenna. After these little argumentative track meets they have, Kyle feels lucky if he hasn't collapsed with emotional exhaustion!

Let's turn our attention now to the second scenario, which offers Kyle a much more tolerable level of intensity. He knows that Kenna has to be true to her personality. She's going to speak her mind and he accepts that reality. Still, there are subtle adjustments she can make in her approach that make all the difference for him. Did you notice the slight change in Kenna's approach when she touches on Kyle's hot-button issue? In the first scenario, she curtly says, "I knew this would happen. The problem is you're just too nice." In the second scenario, however, she adds a couple of very simple but strategic concessions into the mix: "You do things the right way. I love that about you. It's just that I would also love it if just once you would break your own rules . . . just tell someone 'no' for a change." By crafting her words carefully, Kenna accomplishes a great deal. First, she disarms Kyle by acknowledging and expressing appreciation for his strict honesty. Once that olive branch is delivered, she is then able to express her frustrations in a way that Kyle is able to receive.

Kenna goes on to make other subtle adjustments, as does Kyle. In summary, their words in scenario number two are affirming, respectful, and honest, while their words in scenario number one are colored with derision, defensiveness, and sarcasm. By taking the time to understand and adapt to each other's metabolic sensitivities, as they do in scenario number one, they convert conflict into an opportunity to grow closer. They leave the situation knowing that they still have each other's back, in spite of their disagreements. They walk away feeling emotionally safe with one another.

FOOD FOR THOUGHT: Not all conflict can be resolved. Some conflict in relationships is so harmful that it may be necessary to get out in order to be safe.

- *Nearly a third of women in the U.S. have experienced domestic violence (The* Washington Post, *September 8, 2014).*
- *Domestic violence is the leading cause of injury to women between the ages of 15 and 44 in the U.S., more than car accidents, muggings, and rapes combined (*Violence Against Women: A Majority Staff Report, Committee on the Judiciary, United States Senate, 102nd Congress, October 1992, p.3).*

Couple's Quiz: **CONFLICT**

Answer each question by rating the variables of F.I.D. using a number from the scale below. Then ask your partner to do the same. Later, you'll add the total scores to a worksheet in the concluding chapter.

How negatively affected are you by **CONFLICT** in your relationship?

For you . . .

SUBJECT	FREQUENCY	INTENSITY	DURATION	SCORE
Conflict				

For your partner . . .

SUBJECT	FREQUENCY	INTENSITY	DURATION	SCORE
Conflict				

Rating Scale
5 = not affected at all (little to no conflict); **4** = barely affected; **3** = somewhat affected; **2** = definitely affected; **1** = significantly affected; **0** = severely affected

Total Score Key
0–5 = Needs a lot of work; **6–10** = Needs some attention; **11–15** = Doing well

CHAPTER 6

Friends and Family

It's an age-old question for couples: When will you get your fill of family and friends? To clarify, when we say "family" we don't mean your own nuclear family, in which you have the role of parent. This chapter is all about family of origin and extended family members. As for "friends," well, they are just that: friends. So how much is enough? That answer depends on so many personality and family dynamics that it's difficult to answer. To help you get closer to an answer, here are some preliminary questions to consider:

1. How cohesive and active was your family growing up?
2. Was yours "a couple of holidays a year" or an "each and every Sunday" type of family?
3. How close do you feel to your family now? Is it a bedrock of strength and comfort or is it a source of strain and discord?
4. How involved in each other's lives are family members?
5. How many friends did you have in school?
6. Did you enjoy lots of casual friendships or were you locked in deep with one or two close friends?

Let's turn now from the past to the here and now. How does your current family and social life differ from that of your upbringing? As an adult, do you feel somewhat worn out from too much friends and family and all the drama that comes with it? On the flip side, are you failing to get enough quality contact with family members and friends? If so, is your significant other helping or hindering? Encouraging or sabotaging? Answering these questions will help you zero in on what you're accustomed to, how you're built, and what your current love-metabolic needs are for connection to family and friends. These are really critical questions to consider when you're in a serious, long-term relationship, because chances are your partner's answers may vary considerably from yours. Of all the ways a couple must learn to sacrifice and compromise for the good of the relationship, this is perhaps one of the most important and difficult. Just as friends and family can support and strengthen a relationship, they can just as quickly tear a couple apart.

FOOD FOR THOUGHT: Socially isolated people are more than twice as likely to die from heart disease as those with solid social circles (by Justin Worland, "Why Loneliness May Be the Next Big Public-Health Issue," Time.com, March 18, 2015).

CASE IN POINT: JACK AND KATHY

To illustrate how friends and family can go from saving grace to wrecking ball, let's introduce you to the Miller family. Jack Miller, father of two young boys, quite fancied his mother-in-law, at least the version of her that he had known over the first several years of his marriage to her daughter, Kathy. Jack, Kathy and the kids had traveled to the Midwest to see her every summer, sometimes staying up to two weeks. From Jack's point of view, what was *not to like* about her? His mother-in-law was spunky, innovative with activities for the kids, and one heck of a good cook! He always ate well while he was there, and let's face it, quality grandma time meant they could get some quality time *as a couple*. They took full advantage of that time and always went back home feeling closer to one another.

So when Jack's mother-in-law announced that she'd like to reverse things and come out to their place for a couple weeks in the summer, Jack had no problem with it. In fact, he was quite looking forward to it, assuming that he could expect more of the same. If it worked so well in *her* house, why not *his*, he thought. And for several days after her arrival in June, he had no evidence to suggest otherwise. She had unleashed her grandmotherly agenda of frolic and fun on the kids and they were eating it up. She took them to water parks, to the zoo, to pizza . . . . you name it. Kathy got a much needed break from the rigors of kid-raising. Jack got his fill of her mom's fantastic cooking. They were all getting along famously, even if it *were* only going to last for a few more days.

And that's where Jack would be wrong. One night, after serving her amazing lasagna, Jack's mother-in-law made a startling announcement: She intended to stay for the rest of the summer—*if that were OK with them, of course.* Kaboom! Her reasons were complicated, but had something to do with allergies and her doctor's recommendation that she not go back home if at all possible until the early fall. Her announcement ushered in a most profound and awkward silence. Jack looked at Kathy; Kathy looked at Jack. Then, in moment of panic, Jack turned back toward his mother-in-law and impulsively threw her the lifeline she was looking for: "Sure . . . yeah . . . sure . . . absolutely! Of course, you can stay with us! She can stay with us, *right honey*? That will be great, really!"

Fast forward to month number two. For a while, things were going pretty well. Jack's mother-in-law had picked up where she left off, doing a stellar job entertaining the kids, making delicious meals, and even helping clean and organize the house. She gladly undertook many of the more tedious parenting tasks, like bathing and putting the kids to bed. But it wasn't long before things started to change. After a few weeks, the novelty of grandma started wearing thin for the kids and quite frankly, so was being a "full time grandma" for Jack's mother-in-law. They couldn't go to water parks and zoos forever, and soon all that extracurricular activity gave way to long, boring afternoons of watching TV together. Truth be told, the grandma act was getting old and even a bit annoying for her, a fact that she soon began to share in earnest with her daughter.

One night, Jack heard from Kathy for the first time about her mother's growing dissatisfaction. He listened as his wife talked at length about how her mom was beginning to complain that the kids lacked discipline and were far too messy, or how disrespectful they could be and how unmotivated they seemed at times. Her mother apparently went so far as to suggest that they, as parents, were to blame. Kathy struggled to remember exactly how she said it, but it was something to the effect that they were "not going to win any parenting awards any time soon." Jack swallowed hard with that one! It was one thing to get irritated with the kids. That's understandable. Who wouldn't if they spent as much time as she had with them? But this crossed the line. It was a personal attack on the very people who had enough familial charity to consent to her much extended stay! She *was* a guest, after all!

And it got worse from there. The more the summer dragged on, the more Jack's mother-in-law criticized and asserted control. The more she tried to control things, the more Jack and Kathy engaged in conversations like the one above. Soon these conversations turned into small disagreements over what to do, which in turn escalated into full-blown arguments by August. After one of these arguments, Kathy committed one of the cardinal sins for couples—something we call the "travesty of triangulation"—when she commiserated for the first time with her mother about her recent fights with Jack. How ironic was *that*? The original object of Kathy's frustrations—her mom—had now become a refuge from her frustrations.

Throughout the rest of the summer, Kathy confided more and more in her mother and slowly lost her own perspective in the process. Her mother always had such a strong, opinionated, even controlling personality, so the transformation happened seamlessly. It didn't take long for her mother's thinly-veiled criticisms and disparaging observations to find a home in Kathy's mind. Over time, the entire household had gone topsy-turvy, with Kathy and her mother forming an impenetrable alliance and Jack occupying the cursed corner of the family triangle. In fact, the situation became so toxic for Jack that he started confiding in his brother—even staying overnight with him on occasion—which in turn started a whole new "travesty of triangulation" on his part. Every time they talked, Jack got an earful from his brother, which soured him even more about the entire situation. Meanwhile, Kathy was continually getting an earful from her mom. Before long, the lines in the sand were firmly drawn, bringing the summer to a close with tragic consequences. By September, Jack had a new address, his mother-in-law had an invitation to extend her already extended stay and, for the first time, his marriage was in serious trouble.

———————

We hope a family debacle like Jack and Kathy's will never happen to you. Chances are, though, you probably know someone who has fallen into similar traps, whether it be with a family member or a friend. Stories like this one are unfortunately all-too-common, illustrating how powerful friend and family connections sometimes are. Don't misunderstand. As ensnaring as friend and family ties can be, they can also be powerfully *positive*. We are not espousing an anti-friend/family position, here. At the same time, we aren't necessarily advocating *for* increased friend/family connection, either. Only you can decide if it's a good idea to have your mother-in-law move in with you. Who knows, it could be the best decision you ever make as a couple, assuming, of course, things don't spiral as they did for Jack.

What's certain is that friends and family need to be served up in the right portions. Only you can decide how much is too much. Only you can determine how often you need to see them and how long each visit should be. Once you figure that out for yourself—not the easiest task as you traverse down the road of independence into adulthood, by the way—you then have to balance your metabolic needs for friends/family connection with those of your romantic partner.

That's when things can get complicated and precarious! Looking at your needs from a F.I.D. perspective, there is much to consider. Do your cravings for connection closely match your partner's? If not, how wide is the gap? Is he left scratching his head when you tell him you want to go over to your aunt's house for Sunday dinner—*again*? Do you find it annoyingly inconvenient that he consumes all his yearly family calories in one binge visit that lasts for three weeks during the summer? Perhaps your cravings are better satisfied with high-frequency, short-duration contact, while he only gets his fill when it's the other way around. Perhaps you're both lucky enough to agree on the *intensity* front, preferring, for instance, to keep friends and family at a safe distance and limit what you tell them about your personal lives. These are all important questions to ask. With that in mind, let's go ahead and examine each component of F.I.D. in greater detail.

Frequency

Leaving family to start one of your own can be both exhilarating *and* intimidating. Depending on the degree of attachment to your original family, that life transition can also leave you feeling lonely and displaced, whatever the bond you share with your new life partner. Some families are so cohesive—so connected with one another—that it's difficult to imagine how you can shine outside of your fixed place in the family constellation. Other families are more detached, promoting instead a spirit of independence and autonomy rather than interdependence.

It's not uncommon in these types of families to see each sibling move to entirely different locations, often far away from the homestead. The real question here is two-fold: How were your raised and how do you feel about family now? No surprise, couples can be in for some rough weather when their answers to these questions fall on opposite sides of the spectrum.

CASE IN POINT: ROBERT AND VANESSA

So it was for Robert and Vanessa, a couple we knew some time ago. They actually had a solid relationship, sharing much in common. The one thing they didn't share was their appetite for continued family attachments. Robert was from a small family back East and only occasionally connected with his sister and parents, usually over the phone. He would travel to see his parents about once a year. Vanessa was from a very large nuclear and extended Catholic family, 80% of which lived within 20 miles of one another. Their wedding was a major family production, as were all the other national and religious holidays, for that matter.

Robert initially admired how close Vanessa's family members were and was even a bit envious. Over time, though, that envy gave way to irritation and ultimately to desperation. It was one thing to spend every major holiday and life event with them, but it was quite another to acquiesce to the constant barrage of little obligations that chipped away at their time together. Whether they went to her mom's for Sunday dinner, to a family potluck in the park, or to a second cousin's niece's second birthday party, it was slowly eating away at him. In fact, the obligations and gatherings—large and small—occurred so frequently he could hardly remember a single week in their entire existence as a couple in which they were *not* engaging with her family in some way. He simply wasn't getting near enough alone time with his wife!

Eventually, Robert's dissatisfaction reached critical mass and he approached Vanessa with the utmost urgency, explaining to her that if they didn't get some emergency "together time" very soon there would be dire consequences. He even threw out the word divorce. He explained that his life-plan included a marriage *to her*, not her *entire family*. It was a moment of truth for their relationship, for sure! Still, they got through it, as sticky as it was to navigate all the boundary setting and hurt feelings that inevitably followed. Their solution was a compromise that ultimately saved their marriage, underwritten with three main goals: Increase their together-time, commit to Vanessa's family for major holidays and events only, and reach out more to Robert's family members.

This third goal spoke to the importance of one other critical thing to think about when determining the ideal frequency of family contact. It's not just an issue of striking the right balance with your family and your relationship; it is, in all reality, the act of balancing a triangle— your time as a couple versus time with *your family* versus time with *your partner's family*. In Robert's case, he didn't need near as much family contact as Vanessa did to feel connected, but they decided nonetheless that he needed more than he had been getting.

Duration

Interestingly, part of their compromise was also to lengthen the duration of their trips to see Robert's family. While he didn't really need to see his family as often, he felt as though their previous excursions were rushed. In that regard, Robert felt unfulfilled. If they were going to make the effort to go all that way, then why not stay a while? He so much preferred reminiscing and catching up with extended family members in person as opposed to doing so over the phone, but their three to four-day visits limited those opportunities. It always seemed that Robert felt somewhat guilty after leaving, realizing he had failed to fully connect with the few important family members in his life. Understanding the need, Vanessa suggested that they start planning ahead for longer trips. She realized and admitted that she had unknowingly pressured Robert to keep his family visits short, concerned about missing her own family functions. Robert sincerely appreciated and acted on her suggestion.

Intensity

Just as the frequency of Vanessa's family contact was extremely high, so was the intensity of some of her connections, particularly the one she shared with her sister. They spent not only a considerable amount of time together each week, but they were accustomed to swimming in some very deep, personal waters. Over the years there were many personal crises—the threat of divorce, a miscarriage, her husband's lay-off, etc.—that pulled Vanessa deep into her sister's family matters. So, not only was Robert feeling frustrated with the endless number of events and obligations, he was also feeling emotionally neglected. The fact is Vanessa only had so much heart and soul to give, and at times all her emotional reserves were tapped dry just trying to support her sister. That left very little love energy to send Robert's way.

To Robert, the problem was bigger than two emotionally enmeshed sisters embroiled in family drama. It seemed to him that the entire family system had its tentacles into every possible crack and corner of life. The family was very large—brothers, sisters, children, grand-children, even great-grandchildren—and notwithstanding their numbers, most family members lived in the same metropolitan area. On top of that, Vanessa's mother and grandmother were consummate matriarchs with an inexhaustible amount of energy and will-power when it came to family functions. They not only tirelessly organized gatherings like cooking parties, reunions, and ice cream socials, but—at least from Robert's point of view—they also eagerly forged their way into other family members' private business. He remembered one time when Vanessa unwittingly leaked the idea that they were considering the possibility of moving back East, as Robert was up for a promotion and potential transfer. No sooner did she utter the sounds than she was met with a bevy of protests from her mom and grandma. "You wouldn't leave us, would you?" her mother cried, laying the guilt on as thick as her famous garlic-butter spread.

So, yes: Vanessa's family intensity was high by anyone's standard, let alone Robert's. There was no denying that her family had an acute, gravitational pull on all its members. It informed, influenced, and at times, coerced critical personal decisions, such as where to live, when to have children, how many children to have, and of course, how much time to spend with "their side" of the family. It even had the power to reach into less significant areas of life and influence trivial decisions such as what to cook for dinner, what to do for entertainment, and how to spend leisure time.

Most importantly for our discussion, it had the power to completely wear Robert out! It is little wonder why Robert—whose family was far less intense in comparison—felt overwhelmed and overrun. Whatever hard-fought territory he managed to claim in her life, her family always seemed to find a way to seize it back. The good news is that Robert and Vanessa were able to talk through this issue—albeit painfully—and come to an understanding. With a lot of patience, communication, and compromising, they were able to balance their different appetites for family connection with their need for intimate connection as a couple.

Couple's Quiz: **FRIENDS AND FAMILY**

Answer each question by rating the variables of F.I.D. using a number from the scale below. Then ask your partner to do the same. Later, you'll add the total scores to a worksheet in the concluding chapter.

How satisfied are you with the amount and quality of contact with **FAMILY AND/OR FRIENDS**?

For you . . .

SUBJECT	FREQUENCY	INTENSITY	DURATION	SCORE
Friends/Family				

For your partner . . .

SUBJECT	FREQUENCY	INTENSITY	DURATION	SCORE
Friends/Family				

Rating Scale
5 = extremely satisfied; **4** = satisfied; **3** = somewhat satisfied; **2** = somewhat dissatisfied; **1** = dissatisfied; **0** = extremely dissatisfied

Total Score Key
0–5 = Needs a lot of work; **6–10** = Needs some attention; **11–15** = Doing well

How much of a problem for you is your partner's amount and quality of contact with **FAMILY AND FRIENDS**?

For you . . .

SUBJECT	FREQUENCY	INTENSITY	DURATION	SCORE
Friends/Family				

For your partner . . .

SUBJECT	FREQUENCY	INTENSITY	DURATION	SCORE
Friends/Family				

Rating Scale
5 = no problem at all; **4** = it's barely a problem; **3** = it's somewhat of a problem; **2** = it's definitely a problem; **1** = it's a considerable problem; **0** = it's a major problem

Total Score Key
0–5 = Needs a lot of work; **6–10** = Needs some attention; **11–15** = Doing well

CHAPTER 7

Boundaries, Borders and Barricades

Yes, love is full of risk! No doubt you've had your share of falls. Then again, love can give you wings, taking you to new personal heights. When we finally feel safe with that special someone—after we peel away layer after layer of fear—it can be truly freeing. But the freedom to safely soar is only as good as the wings it rides on. Those wings are made of a very precious material called trust, and trust, ironically, can be a very fragile thing. That's why couples need to take great care to safeguard it. Once it weakens and cracks, it's only a matter of time before the relationship takes a nose dive.

Sure, you've heard artists on the radio offer their sage relationship advice to overly anxious lovers over the years. Sting, for example, once pleaded, "If you love someone, set them free." .38 Special (if they can be considered experts in love and relationships) proclaimed, "Hold on loosely, but don't let go. If you cling too tightly, you're gonna lose control." True. All true. It's never good to be clingy and controlling. That erodes trust, as well. Just talk with the Germans in Berlin, where not so long ago a very literal wall of fear was erected to exert strict control over who could enter or leave what was then East Berlin. It stood for a good while as a seemingly impregnable concrete expression of power and control, but in the end it was knocked to the ground along with the stifling political system it represented.

Oppressive control represents only one extreme on the trust-busting continuum. On the other side lies the problems associated with too much freedom: poorly defined boundaries with those outside the relationship. You wouldn't hesitate to talk about personal safety with a young child in your care. The rules would be clearly defined and communicated: Unsupervised play is allowed in the backyard only; no climbing the fence to retrieve lost balls; ask permission before leaving the house, and so on. You also wouldn't fail to protect your beloved family canine, if not through the power of words then through the power of invisible fence technology, a retractable leash, or some other measure. Yet there it is: Many couples fail to have even a rudimentary discussion about setting healthy boundaries for their relationship, failing to realize that the emotional consequences can be severe.

Granted, it's probably not a fun topic to broach with your significant other! It's a sensitive conversation at best, an explosive one at worst. Ironically, it's not simply the volatile nature of the subject that discourages couples from talking about it; it's also a tough subject to tackle because so many people are out of touch with *their own* personal needs and wants in this area. Yes, even the issue of healthy boundaries is subject to love-metabolic tolerance levels and appetites. We'll explore this throughout the chapter, but suffice it to say, we see so many couples wind up in a real mess when their love-metabolic differences surface in this area. The problem is not so much that differences exist as there isn't nearly enough self-awareness and communication about those differences. It really is a conversation that needs to happen again and again. Without honest dialogue, there's no chance for understanding, compromise, and establishing clear expectations for how each should behave when it comes to contact with people outside the relationship.

So again, establishing healthy boundaries is not about building your own Berlin Wall; it's not about forbidding exploration, expression, and interaction with the outside world of family, friends, and co-workers. On the contrary, healthy boundaries are tailor-made, permeable borders with enough safeguards to preserve trust while still allowing space to breath. These borders, created through compromise and based on each partner's unique appetites and tolerance levels, are all about preserving trust at its most basic level and strengthening emotional attachments. They should not be driven by irrational fears and "jealousy," but rather by a sincere desire to protect what's most vulnerable and precious deep within you. You are, after all, trusting someone with your heart!

FOOD FOR THOUGHT: 60% of all married individuals in the U.S. will engage in infidelity at some point in their marriage (1997 research from Buss and Shackelford in "Facts and Statistics About Infidelity" at www.truthaboutdeception.com).

But that begs the question: Should you ever trust someone with your heart in the first place? Should you place your hopes for happiness and fulfillment in the hands of another? Have you not heard over and over that the power to achieve happiness lies *within* you—that it can't be delivered by anyone or anything outside of you? Well, we've heard it too and agree whole-heartedly. Ultimately, you *are* accountable for your own happiness and you have to be right with yourself before you can be right for *someone else*. Still, we are inherently social creatures and the desire for romantic attachment is in our DNA. With that in mind, we firmly believe that most people realize their full potential for happiness within loving, committed, romantic partnerships.

This is where things get tricky: We just told you to look within to find happiness, but we also said that your greatest happiness comes through surrendering your heart to another. In other words, be self-reliant and *independent* as much as possible, but be *dependent* if you really want to be happy. Confusing? Paradoxical? Well, yes it is. But take heart; there is middle ground to be had—a compromise between the two extremes that provides couples a safe place to land.

The late Steven R. Covey, in his motivational masterpiece, *The Seven Habits of Highly Effective People*, regarded this compromise as the sweet-spot for human connection, referring to it as "interdependence." In short, while dependence makes us too vulnerable and independence leaves us too disconnected, interdependence strikes the delicate balance between the two. We need to know we can do it—that we can count on ourselves to survive and thrive. On the other hand, we crave love and want so much to feel safe enough to give our hearts to another. Interdependence is a place in which people rely on and trust their romantic relationships enough to go to the next level of happiness and fulfillment, without sacrificing that sense of self and personal security they may have worked so hard to obtain.

KEEPING THE WOLVES AT BAY

In a nutshell, what we've established so far is that love is built on trust and trust must be safeguarded. When trust is compromised, you inevitably lose that feeling of safety that's so vital to forming the secure attachments that make us the happiest we can be. With that in mind, build some fences in your relationship, if you haven't already started! If you have, then it's always good to mend and reinforce the ones you've got in place. If you're curious as to what these fences are designed to protect your relationship *from*, allow us to mention a few wolves that have been known to cross the line dressed as sheep.

FOOD FOR THOUGHT: Men are more likely than women to cheat. However, men are less likely to leave their marriages when having an affair (www.truthaboutdeception.com)

Exes

Ex-wives, ex-husbands, ex-girlfriends, ex-boyfriends, ex-friends-with-benefits—they all present a real risk to the security of your relationship. Even if there is no chance in hell either of you would make a move in that direction, the mere presence of an ex often causes some level of discomfort and anxiety. Look, we're not suggesting at all that you have to categorically discard all trappings of your former romantic life. Sometimes, you just don't have a real choice, as your ex may be the mother or father of your children or may share ties with others in your inner circle of friends and colleagues. In these cases, continued contact is inevitable.

In other cases, you do, in fact, have a choice. Do you choose to remain "friends" with former romantic interests? If so, to what extent do you stay in contact? Do you talk on the phone occasionally, randomly text each other about trivial matters from time to time, or actually meet-up in person at a local coffee shop once a month? Whatever the answers to these questions, the real question is this: How do these choices affect the intimate bond you enjoy with your partner? It's not such a simple question, after all. While you may trust your own feelings implicitly, you may find that your partner is feeling less than secure. It's absolutely imperative that you get on the same page with one another when it comes to contact with exes. Whether you decide on limited contact or no contact at all, you better make sure you agree on *something*.

Coming to such an agreement well before the holidays could have really helped Martin and Paula. Martin had one of those "nice-guy" personalities and was determined not to hurt other people's feelings. This was true for his ex's feelings, as well. He was proud of the fact that he could move on from past relationships without the bitterness, petty jealousy, and aversion so many other displaced lovers often exhibit following their break-ups. Unlike them, he had a way of looking back on his romantic past with gratitude, regardless of how messy things got or how painfully things ended. To Martin, if exes were important to him at one time, there would always be a small place in his heart for them. That's why he had no qualms about staying in touch—within reason—with some of his exes. In fact, on some level he felt he *owed it to them*.

But Martin's appetite and tolerance levels for contact with exes was very different from Paula's. She had no appetite for it at all. She had no desire to connect with exes, plain and simple, nor did she want Martin doing it. Still, she knew his heart. She liked how big it was and how much it was willing to give her. That's part of what made her fall in love with him in the first place. Then again, his heart was in some ways too big for comfort; it simply had too much space for too many people, especially past lovers that Paula couldn't help but find threatening, in spite of Martin's many reassurances to the contrary. But the rub for her wasn't entirely about the underlying fear of infidelity. To Paula, Martin's tinkering with past lovers was at the very least an indication he was living in the past, something she found unattractive and, in some ways, unhealthy. At worst, it was a sign that he was not *really* in love with her. Either way, it obviously wasn't good for their relationship.

As kind-hearted as Martin may have been, kindness was in short supply when things came to a head one afternoon during a trip to see relatives over the holidays. With a long layover and time on their hands, Paula decided to confront Martin, once and for all, about the texting he had been doing with his previous girlfriend. Martin felt blindsided. He simply wasn't ready for something like this, especially at a time when feelings of good will and holiday cheer usually prevail. He was feeling really good with her at that moment, but then she just had to bring it up—*all over again*. She reiterated her reasoning, shared her feelings, and preached her usual sermon about the dangers of loose boundaries. None of it was news. Martin retorted with predictable self-defense tactics, which Paula had heard more than a few times. He re-asserted that the content of his recent texting with his ex was not even remotely of a personal nature. Most of it had to do with football news and scores, nothing more. Exasperated, he asked her, again, why she felt so threatened by it—why she simply couldn't believe there was nothing romantic anymore between them. They were just friends—and there was nothing treacherous about answering a friendly text or two.

While they had bantered this about on previous occasions, this little go-round was different. For some reason, their love-metabolic disconnect over boundaries had reached a fever-pitch. She grew more and more anxious and desperate as they talked, while he felt more and more attacked and controlled. Soon the talking gave way to barely veiled shouting, a few choice vocabulary words, and a second-leg flight in total silence. That's right! They didn't share a single word with one another as they traveled the final two hours to their destination. Not exactly the best way to get into the holiday spirit, was it?

FOOD FOR THOUGHT: When a wife cheats on her husband, she is more likely to have an emotional affair. Women are less likely to have one night stands than men (www.truthaboutdeception.com).

So how could they have prevented this love-metabolic meltdown? First, let's acknowledge the fact that Paula had confronted the subject more than once. That doesn't mean they got close to a resolution, however. They clearly didn't. The problem presented itself like a small itch that got progressively worse until it developed into a full-blown rash. By the end, all they had was inflammation worthy of a trip to the ER. Still, give credit to Paula. She tried. Then again, she didn't really know what she could reasonably expect of Martin, nor did she know the best way to ask for it. He, on the other hand, was operating in oblivion. He understood and sensed she wasn't comfortable, but he just couldn't get why. It was so foreign to him. Replying to the text of an old friend (an ex-lover notwithstanding), seemed as natural as breathing.

As big as the divide was, however, this altercation really shook them up, so much so that arriving at a solution was now a matter of utmost urgency. Paula, for one, realized that she could no longer just complain her way to change. She had to look within for answers, and in doing so she was able to clarify her motives, identify her fears, and better own her feelings. With greater self-understanding, she could then approach Martin in a way that was less critical of *him* and more focused on her own feelings. For example, she could say fewer things like, "Why is it so important that you talk to an old girlfriend about football?," and more things like, "I know staying connected to people is natural for you, but sometimes I just feel uncomfortable with it." This put Martin less on the defensive. In fact, this small adjustment proved to be ingenious because it elicited the very ingrained, empathetic response that made him so willing to respond to exes in the first place. Once she "owned" her insecure feelings and expressed them as such, he naturally came to her rescue with a desire to make the pain stop. She was the *last* person he would ever want to hurt, after all.

With the focus off of his "poor judgment" and squarely on Paula's discomfort, Martin realized that it didn't matter what her reasons were or even whether she had any good reasons at all. His actions were hurting her and that was enough. With that in mind, Martin made the decision to go ahead and contact this particular ex and explain—as kindly as he could—that he needed to cease communication with her out of respect for Paula. It didn't end there, however. After he did, he and Paula had the kind of long, productive discussion they desperately needed from the beginning. With their defenses down and their hearts open, they discussed the entire issue of contact with exes, identified the sore spots, and made some real compromises that strengthened their relationship.

Colleagues and Co-workers

Do you find yourself talking a lot to your partner about people at work? "He did this . . . she did that." "He's so funny . . . she's so cool." As you recite your amusing tales about the happenings at your job, how sure are you that your partner is entirely comfortable with the level of familiarity you have with people he or she *doesn't really know*? Yes, we're sure your partner understands the need for good working relationships and that some of these naturally morph into friendships. It's completely reasonable and natural. But it's the unknown that's scary. "How funny *is* he?" "How cool *is* she?" "Cooler or funnier than *me*?" Even if it doesn't immediately rise to the level of suspicion, a small seed of concern can sprout over time and grow into something that eventually comes between you.

Don't overestimate yourself, either. Far too many unsuspecting souls have found themselves in precarious situations at work because they failed to take precautions. Of course, it hardly ever starts out as a conscious effort to romantically attach to a co-worker. It's usually very subtle and gradual, but it's almost always perpetuated by loose boundaries and poor personal discipline. Do you go to lunch with colleagues? If so, do you occasionally venture out one-on-one? Do those lunches naturally drag on longer and longer because the conversations grow increasingly personal? Have any work partners told you that you're "easy to talk to" or have they shared that "no one gets them" like you do? Sound familiar? If so, get out the hammer, nails, and post-digger because it's high time to start building a fence. It's sad but true: Even something as insignificant as going out for food can be a slippery slope. A couple of wrong steps just might cause an avalanche of personal problems.

Let's get even more slippery. Do you sometimes hit happy hour with co-workers? If so, are there enough of you there to realistically call it "group bonding," or does it often turn into a drunken gathering of just a few overly-friendly work companions with their guards down? Do you plan ahead of time for how long you'll let yourself be there and how many drinks you'll allow yourself to consume? Either way, does your partner know what you're up to and are they *really* OK with your plans? Have they personally met these people you occasionally spend your after-work hours with? Don't be fooled by how harmless after-work fraternizing can seem. We know people that eventually lost their jobs and jeopardized their marriages because of indiscretions committed in this way.

But if happy hour isn't slippery enough, let's talk about the bob-sled run of relationship disasters called the "business trip." This one can be a certified home wrecker! Invariably, boundaries should most certainly be tightened while on the road. Don't travel with anyone but yourself? Don't travel with anyone interesting or enticing? Fair enough. People in your home office aren't the only source of concern, though. How about colleagues from other offices? What about all those hours with established clients? How about strangers you meet in the hotel lobby, bar, or restaurant? If your business trip is like many others, you can expect to indulge in at least a modest amount of local entertainment. Let's face it, that's often the "fun" part that makes business travel worth the hassle. The problem is those "fun" times can easily cause you to lower your guard. In fact, travel, by its very nature, has a way of knocking your healthy routines and habits out of orbit. You're eating out all the time, meeting new people, socializing with others you rarely see, and staying overnight in strange beds. It's really not a stretch to say that you're just a few bad decisions away from sharing that strange bed with someone else!

FOOD FOR THOUGHT: There are 17 different types of affairs a person can have. One of them is the "accidental affair," caused by, you guessed it, poor boundaries (research by Mira Kirshenbaum in her book, *When Good People Have Affairs*, St. Martin's Griffin, 2009.).

Neighbors

Let's suppose you're one of *those* people. "Like a good neighbor," you're always *there* for the neighbors on your street. You've got the right personality and just enough know-how. You're approachable, helpful, and just can't help but say "yes." What's not to like about *that*?

Generally speaking, it's a good thing to be accessible—a real asset. In some instances, though, it can present boundary problems if you're not careful. Saying "yes" too many times to the wrong neighbor can lead to eroding boundaries, poor choices, and eventual indiscretions.

That's what happened to Randy. He was happily married, and he and his wife and two teenage kids moved into a cozy neighborhood. As he would soon learn, however, it proved to be a bit *too cozy*. Self-employed, he worked odd hours at home while his wife did a steady 8-5 at her office in town. Thus Randy found himself home alone much of the time. That fact wasn't lost on his neighbor, Claire, a divorced, single mom who struggled to stay afloat. At first it wasn't a big deal. She would look up and notice him driving past while she was watering her flowers. She would smile and wave. He would wave back. After so many times, Randy began to slow the car, roll down the window, and say hello. Soon a few harmless greetings turned into brief banter about the weather, school stuff, or neighborhood gossip.

Although it seemed insignificant at the time, the stakes were raised dramatically one day during a routine two- to three-minute neighborly exchange. Randy noticed that Claire was using the wrong kind of fertilizer and asked her about it. She replied that she really didn't know what she was doing, but that she remembered her ex-husband doing something with the lawn to make it greener. Randy started to explain a little about grass types and seasonal maintenance cycles, but then trailed off midsentence as the thought hit him. A little voice in his mind whispered that it would be crossing a line somehow, but every chivalrous bone in his body urged his mouth to form the words. "You know what, I've got the right fertilizer in the garage," he replied. With those simple words his role shifted imperceptibly from friendly neighbor to care-giving rescuer. It was so seamless that neither of them noticed.

Once they crossed that neighborly Rubicon, so to speak, things quickly escalated. That's not to say that they were entirely aware of their budding emotional connection at first. They were far too distracted by a steady stream of busy work—work that never seemed to end. He would start fertilizing, for instance, then notice a sprinkler head that wasn't working properly. She would say, "Oh, don't worry about it. It's no big deal."

He would protest, "No, it needs to be replaced. It won't take much to get it fixed up." One small thing would lead to something bigger, and so on.

Pretty soon, Randy found himself over there almost daily, and the more he knew about her, the more he sympathized with her situation— living life as a single mom with limited income, time and support. He hadn't crossed that line of infidelity in his heart yet, for certain, but he couldn't deny the strange gravitational pull Claire had on him. That pull became so strong that he would linger in her yard even after he was finished helping her. That's when Randy truly began to recognize that he was swimming in dangerous waters. With each smile, heartfelt thank you, and iced tea she offered, Randy could feel himself drifting past the divider that marks the transition to the deep end of the pool. But he was too dazed to pull himself to safety.

Claire soon felt comfortable enough to start knocking on Randy's door for help or advice and it was only a matter of time before Randy invited her in. Once he did, their relationship left the "outside" world of gardening and entered the inner-world of homes and hearts. But what else could he do? It felt so natural, in spite of the little voice within that told him not to let her cross the threshold. All that time spent in Claire's company had made its mark. Too many hours, too many conversations, and too much face-to-face caused them to form a bond, one that ultimately defied their ability to adhere to or even fully recognize healthy boundaries.

Can you guess the rest from here? Not so fast. It doesn't quite end the way you might expect. Yes, Randy's wife (Sara) discovered his emotional affair. Fortunately for him, the discovery occurred before he could manage to obliterate any remaining barriers to infidelity. It happened one afternoon when Sara left work early because she was feeling ill. Now, to be fair, she wasn't entirely in the dark about Randy's activities with Claire. To his credit, he had freely informed her about his neighborly service project. Still, she had no idea of the extent, nor did she suspect that an emotional affair was sprouting alongside Claire's new and improved lawn. At any rate, when she turned down her street, she saw the two of them embracing, right there in Claire's driveway! They weren't even trying to hide it! Almost in disbelief, Sara slowed the vehicle as she passed. She glanced over and caught Randy completely off guard. He immediately broke the embrace, looked awkwardly at Claire, and then rushed over nervously to Sara's passing car.

Randy and Sara had a very long conversation shortly thereafter. As you might imagine, she expressed feelings of betrayal. She couldn't believe her eyes. What was he thinking? He replied by explaining what "really happened"—that Claire had just hung up the phone with a relative, who informed her that her aunt had passed away. Without thinking she just threw her arms around him and he reciprocated. That was it— *really*! But then Sara knew there *had* to be more to it. While she mostly accepted his explanation, she nonetheless refused to back off her point that Randy had crossed the line with Claire in that moment. She then asked Randy if he actually had some sort of "feelings" for Claire. Randy swallowed hard, feeling convicted by the small nugget of truth. Yes, he admitted he had slipped into some sort of attraction or fascination with her, but he also adamantly reaffirmed that he had no intention of jeopardizing his marriage any further. He expressed how sorry he was for letting her down. Once the intense feelings subsided some, they began piecing together a story of how poor boundary-setting turned good intentions into careless mistakes.

Let's look at Sara's situation from a love-metabolic perspective. After this betrayal of trust, she needed more assurances than usual. True, she was one to naturally trust and allow her husband a considerable amount of freedom. She *was* OK with loosely defined boundaries. Not anymore, though. Because of this incident with Claire, her tolerance levels changed dramatically—at least for a period of time. On the flip-side, the incident was also a huge wake-up call for Randy. He realized that in spite of his best intentions, he was in reality a vulnerable, emotional human being who over time was capable of succumbing to the stealthy forces of attraction. Looking back, he could identify where he went wrong and at what points along the way he could have built some sturdy relationship fences—instead of fixing sprinklers.

From that point on, Randy worked full-time repairing the damaged trust with his wife. As might be imagined, he had some real work to do. Of course, the first item of business was to immediately cut things off with Claire. Randy called her up and had a very respectful chat with her about the need to put healthy boundaries back in place. She agreed and also apologized to him for her part in letting things get out of hand.

Sara was happy he willingly made that move, but she didn't want him to be anyone but himself—that kind-hearted, helpful guy she fell in love with and married. She didn't expect him to be cold to his neighbors, in other words. So they decided together that smiling, waving, and even exchanging a few cordial words would be acceptable should he happen to pass Claire in the future. That was only natural, she thought. Then again, they both agreed that all deliberate contact should cease and that Claire would simply have to look elsewhere when she needed help. Randy, in good faith, also said he would text Sara more from home to fill her in on his activities during the day, let her know he was thinking about her, and express his love for her. It was a good compromise that created safeguards and increased communication. Yes, the process hurt some, but in the end, Randy and Sara worked it out and managed to grow closer to one another.

Social Media

Randy may have crossed his boundaries the old fashioned way, neighbor-to-neighbor, but far more indiscretions these days are instigated through the use of social media. There's no place where boundaries are fuzzier than cyberspace. We hear so many stories of infidelity, emotional or otherwise, that spring from Facebook, Instagram, Twitter, and even Linkedin˚. Let's be clear: social media is not inherently the enemy. It's the concept of "friendship at the click of a button" that's so dangerous. The sheer volume of cyber-social contact any one person can reasonably manage these days is staggering. What's more, for every exchange you have with friends, schoolmates, co-workers, and extended family members, you get 10 unsolicited suggestions to connect with other people you had all but forgotten about. Thus we have an unprecedented number of people in our lives with an unprecedented ability to instantly connect with them.

Needless to say, this represents a serious and growing threat to healthy relationship boundaries. Simply put, it's easier than ever to get into trouble. It just doesn't take any work. At least Randy had to sweat a little. But with social media, all it takes is one "friend" suggestion, a glance at a profile picture, and a flood of memories from high school to completely undo a couple. Sure, we might be oversimplifying the steps to relational disaster, but in reality it doesn't take much for a small, cyber-distraction to turn into a full-blown "e-affair."

FOOD FOR THOUGHT: Men are more likely to have online affairs than are women (Jane Weaver in an iVillage survey; NBC.com).

How many times have we heard it? A woman three years post-divorce sees the image of her old college crush in her online friend's photo album. Now in times past—back in the *old school* days of tangible photo albums—she might have seen his face, felt the rush of reverie, and wondered how his life turned out. Was he married? Was he happy? Did he ever think about her after that? Answering these questions, however, would have required a lot of digging—too much digging, probably, for most people. Thus the exercise in nostalgia would have hit a dead end.

But in this digital world we live in, she sees his image and likely notices that his name is tagged to the photo. That tag turns out to be a link to his personal page and without thinking, she clicks through and views his profile picture. He looks better than ever! But then there's that cover photo of his wife and kids. No worries—she doesn't intend to cross any lines with anyone. She'll just give a quick look at some of his photos and be done in a couple minutes. But in truth, a quick look turns into a few hours of devouring photographs and posts, and it isn't long before she's hooked all over again. The funny thing is she has no idea she's hooked.

Then the moment of truth. There it is: the "message" button, just begging to be clicked. Just a short *hey there and hello*, she thinks. Yeah, that would probably be just fine. It's not like she's going to actually relive college all over again. He's moved on, obviously, and so has she. They probably wouldn't feel the same way about each other anyhow, even if they *were* given a second chance. Yeah, just a quick little harmless message will do!

Now it's his turn. He gets her message and is instantly ecstatic—"instantly" because his smart phone is of course fully synched with all his various social media accounts. He replies right away with some *OMG*s and *LOL*s. She's thrilled to receive his reply. They chit-chat from there, quite innocently. They share a few stories and laughs from back in the day. After 10 minutes or so, they sign off, mutually expressing how great it was to connect after all these years.

Not surprisingly, he then goes through the exact same process she did. He checks out her posts—even comments on a few. He forgot how sharp and funny she was. He gets a real kick out of reading her responses to others' comments. Then he views her photos. One by one, he gets drawn in. He forgot how pretty she was. Finally he stumbles upon a photo album entitled, "College Days," and finds an old picture of the two of them, one that hits his brain like a bolt of lightning. Twenty-five years is reduced to a passing moment. He can see, taste, and feel that night like it had just happened.

You don't have to be as smart as Mark Zuckerberg to know what happens from there. As with all emotional affairs from the dawn of time, one thing leads to another. It's just that in our scenario, one thing follows another at 32 bits per second. Sure, the story is the same as it ever was: He knew me when—before life got complicated; she understands me and respects who I really am, *unlike my wife*, etc. It's just that now, contact doesn't have to wait for a chance encounter at the grocery store. It doesn't have to wait for just the right moment of privacy for a phone call. It's right there just a click away. We truly have the world at our fingertips, but for many couples it has unfortunately become a world of trouble.

Save yourself from all that trouble by talking openly about social media with your partner. Get to know one another's appetites and tolerance levels for cyber-connection. You may have 50 online friends while your partner may have 550. It simply might not be an important form of communication to you. Or, perhaps, it's the other way around. In either case, you need to come up with some solid ground rules if you truly want to prevent someone from hacking into your relationship. Depending on your personal preferences and experience with infidelity in relationships, you might consider establishing some boundaries like these:

1. "Friending" old flames is ordinarily off limits but could be permissible in some circumstances if both agree on it. Direct contact or commenting on a post, however, is *not* OK.

2. Commenting or posting on a married friend's wall is allowable as long as the content is not of a sensitive, personal nature and your partner is also friends with the person or couple. Direct, private messaging is off-limits unless the message serves a functional purpose (sharing details of an upcoming reunion, etc.)

3. No "trolling" (surfing) aimlessly through online profiles listed on Facebook and other social media sites (it may seem more innocent than trolling through an online dating site, but as they say, curiosity

killed the cat). Read and send your messages, review your notifications, and log out.

That gives you some good suggestions, but keep the conversation going. Don't underestimate the power that smart phones and blue screens have on your relationship! Take the time to talk it out and set some healthy boundaries around social media. Get specific and clear about your expectations for one another. Don't leave it up to intuition or common sense. Social media is far too sneaky.

START BUILDING YOUR FENCES TOGETHER

Now that you have a healthy appreciation of the various threats to your relationship and the kinds of havoc they can wreak (e.g., shattered trust, affairs, separation and divorce), it's time to start creating healthy boundaries. Make no mistake, it's a conversation that will fully occur over time, but it never hurts to actually make a plan to start it. Go out first and have some fun. Enjoy each other. Then, when feelings are at their best, sit down and begin the dialogue. You may want to structure your conversation using the following steps:

1. Start by identifying any relationships your partner has that bother, threaten, or make you uncomfortable in any way (e.g., an ex with whom he/she has a long history).

2. Identify the emotional reasons you feel threatened. Peel away the surface emotions like jealously and anger until you get to the root feeling or fear (e,g., "I fear I'm just not interesting enough for you.")

3. Share these fears and feelings with your partner as openly as possible. Own them. Don't use blaming language or make demands. Just let them hang out there, fully exposed to the light of day. Trust your partner to respect your feelings and fears; they will be trusting you with theirs, after all.

4. Take each relationship your partner has identified and ask two questions: 1. What important purpose does communication with this person serve? 2. How much emotional stress does it cause my partner? You have to weigh these two things to determine what to keep, what to throw out, and how to compromise. If, for instance, your partner identifies your ex-husband as a problem relationship for him, you may have little choice about contact with your ex. You have certain things you have to talk about, namely your kids. So perhaps the answer lies not in eliminating contact, but rather in limiting it strictly to business matters, for example. That might be enough to relieve some of the tension between you and your partner. On the other hand, if your partner's uneasy feelings are the result of occasional texts to an old high-school boyfriend who has absolutely no impact on your daily life, you may decide that the negative effects outweigh the negligible positives.

5. After weighing it all out, make plans to eliminate contact that just isn't worth the strain and compromise on everything else. With enough patience and will, you can find some middle-ground to stand on.

6. Reestablish your property lines! This is where you agree on rules to prevent future trespassing. One athletically inclined couple we know made a rule that they would only hire same-sex personal trainers. Another couple that frequently carpooled agreed that they would never ride alone with a member of the opposite sex. Yet another couple decided that communication with their ex-spouses should be confined to e-mails where possible. In the end, it's entirely up to you what's appropriate. Your ideas may change over time, but the fact that you're engaged in the process of establishing boundaries is a very healthy thing. Over time, you'll learn one another's love-metabolic needs and tolerance levels and reach a compromise that really works.

Couple's Quiz: **BOUNDARIES**

Answer each question by rating the variable of F.I.D. using a number from the scale below. Then ask your partner to do the same. Later, you'll add the total scores to a worksheet in the concluding chapter.

How serious are your partner's **BOUNDARY PROBLEMS?**

For you . . .

SUBJECT	FREQUENCY	INTENSITY	DURATION	SCORE
Boundaries				

For your partner . . .

SUBJECT	FREQUENCY	INTENSITY	DURATION	SCORE
Boundaries				

Rating Scale
5 = no real problems; **4** = a few minor problems; **3** = moderate problems;
2 = notable problems; **1** = significant problems; **0** = extreme problems

Total Score Key
0–5 = Needs a lot of work; **6–10** = Needs some attention; **11–15** = Doing well

PART II

CHAPTER 8

"Love Languages, Meet Love Metabolism"

Sometimes a book comes out that therapists find indispensable in their practices, the kind that provides fresh insight and sheds new light on common, relationship challenges. For us, one of these books was Gary Chapman's ground-breaking work, *The Five Love Languages*. There's not a week that goes by that we're not referring to it in some way in our work with couples. If you don't own your own copy, get one. Whether or not you have the book, you've likely been exposed to the concepts.

That's what happened with Jennifer. Do you remember Jon and Jennifer from chapter 1? She was the one who was satisfied with the frequency of the communication with her husband, Jon, but was dissatisfied with the duration and intensity of their discussions. Anyway, she heard some of her girlfriends using the Love Language terminology during one of their weekend get-aways. She asked about what she was hearing, and the group introduced her to the book. She quickly purchased her own copy. Like so many before her, her mind took hold of an entirely new perspective on relationship satisfaction. Page by page, she began to consider the idea that love needs to be communicated to her in a way that resonates with her. Applying that concept to her relationship with Jon, she realized she needed his love to be spoken in a "language" she could understand.

As the chapters unfolded, she discovered that the language of love is spoken in five very different but effective ways. First, she read about the need some people have for *words of affirmation*. These are often words of encouragement—verbal compliments offered either in private or in front of others. Ideally, words of affirmation are delivered kindly, in a spirit of humility and appreciation.

Next, Jennifer learned that some people feel most cherished when their significant other spends *quality time* with them. This time may be spent engaging in shared activities or hobbies, taking a moment to sit down together and talk about the day's events, or embarking on romantic adventures. For others, words and time are nice, but don't go nearly as far as a well-conceived, well-timed *gift*.

Jennifer's understanding continued to expand from there. She learned that some people prefer to show and receive love through *acts of service*. While Jennifer understood that she was desperately missing genuine communication and verbal affirmations from Jon, she readily acknowledged and appreciated the thoughtful things he did for her, such as washing her car unexpectedly, placing all her mail in a special stack off to the side, and keeping on top of all the bills so she didn't have to worry about tedious financial details.

Finally, Jennifer explored the power that *physical touch* holds for some people, looking at both the "explicit" kind of touch, which requires time and concentration (back rubs, kissing, foreplay, and beyond) and the "implicit" category, defined by impromptu displays of physical affection (sitting close, brushing shoulders, spontaneous kiss on the cheek).

Once Jennifer had finished reading *The Five Love Languages*, she had gained an incredible amount of insight into *what* was missing in her relationship with Jon. On the top of her list? Words! She needed communication, both in the form of sincere affirmations and quality conversation. But for Jennifer, that was just the start. If you'll remember, once she shared her insights with Jon, he made a concerted effort to fill the need by communicating with her much more frequently. Still, Jennifer came to realize that while Jon's attempts directly addressed the issue of *what* and *how often*, they failed to give attention to two equally important matters: *how long* and *how much* (two of the three components of F.I.D.). In love metabolic terms, Jon heard the order correctly and served her the right entrée. It's just that he quickly sent her on her way with an undersized to-go box when she was hoping to dine by candlelight!

And thus *Love Metabolism* meets *Love Languages*! Familiar as we were with the ideas in Chapman's book, we quickly realized how our concept could help couples satisfy their hunger for love by building on a solid love-language foundation. That's why we decided to devote an entire section to the topic. We'll start by examining *words of affirmation*, paying particular attention to how a person's appetite for such words can be affected by several variables. We'll turn our attention next to *quality time* and how the word "quality" is defined so differently, depending on whom you ask. Then, after making the case that not all *gifts* are equal and not all *acts of service* are truly appreciated for what they are, we'll finish the discussion with a "sensitive" topic that has spawned volumes of books all on its own: *touch*. Specifically, we'll consider how the temperamental desire for touch is influenced by factors such as timing, location, preferences, culture, and personal history.

FOOD FOR THOUGHT: Get a copy of the book. *The Five Love Languages: How to Express Heartfelt Commitment to Your Mate* (Gary D. Chapman, Northfield Publishing, Chicago, 1995).

CHAPTER 9

Filling Up on Affirming Words

Words: We all use and need them. It's one of the markers that separates us most from other species on the planet. Of all the kinds of words we send back and forth, *words of affirmation* are among the most important. We all like to be reminded, to some degree or another, that we're appreciated, desired and loved. We simply perform and feel better when we hear it. Children, in particular, feed off of praise, which is needed for optimal cognitive and emotional development. So while words of affirmation can be powerful, our point is that they ultimately need to be administered in the right doses, at the right time. What's more, they need to push the right buttons in order for them to work their magic. What ultimately does the trick to make someone feel loved, however, depends on a lot of things. We'll consider four variables that affect a person's love-metabolic needs for affirming words:

1. Gender
2. Self-esteem
3. Family culture
4. Relationship-specific dynamics

GENDER

No surprise, your gender can influence your appetite for words of affirmation. Of course, we acknowledge that not all men are exactly alike, just as we know that not all women share the same craving for words. People are more complicated than that. We get it! As we mentioned in chapter two, however, most men say less than their female companions. By the same token, most men need less communication to feel safe and secure in their relationships. Now, that's not to say there aren't some chatty men out there, but the odds are they don't connect words *with love* in quite the same way a woman does.

Still, contrary to the suspicions of some women, men *are* human and therefore share the need to feel loved and affirmed. While most women crave heart-felt expressions that make them feel adored, missed or desired, words of affirmation for men aren't necessarily best delivered as direct expressions of *love*. Securing your place in his heart may be much more effectively accomplished through carefully crafted words that make him feel *competent* and *respected,* rather than "loved." Put another way, instead of telling him you "love him," you would probably reach the mark better by saying you "love him *for the man that he is!*" This is primal, to say the least. Let's not kid ourselves: There's still a caveman inside every guy, one that wants to feel revered for slaying the metaphorical wooly mammoths of life and bringing home the proverbial bacon—well, *some* kind of meat, anyway. Trapped in an evolutionary time warp, he yearns in his bones to be appreciated for how strong, capable, brave and resourceful he is.

Irretrievably primal as men may be, they still have a heart. Certainly, most men will react positively to, "I love you." The expression should feel good to any man with a pulse. With that in mind, go ahead and say it whenever you feel the urge. Then again, the question here is how deep and how far do those words *really* go? Instead of bouncing words of love off his forehead, as your feminine inner-voice might tell you to do, try instead to locate and push his masculine buttons—the ones that link to feeling accomplished, successful and capable. Specifically, let him know that you notice how hard he works and express to him how much his sacrifices mean to you when he makes them. Give him the assurance that you respect what talents and expertise he brings to your partnership. When he makes a stand to defend you, even in the slightest of circumstances, express to him how supported and protected you feel (this one may have the same powerful effect on a man as chocolate has on a woman). Jump on the chance to point out how resourceful he is when he quickly solves a problem at home. If he does something well, make him feel like he did it even better! In short, if you'll take the dive into the male mind and try a few of these suggestions, you will be amazed at how quickly they lead you to your end goal: Affirming and strengthening your love.

To all you male readers, let us simply say that if you don't already know the truth about women and words of affirmation, then you've been living under a rock. It's as obvious as all those romantic comedies make it out to be: Most women need words that make them feel loved, just as they need oxygen to live. The strategy for delivering these messages is no mystery, either. Just tell her straight up and from the heart. Not a wordsmith? No worries. The actual words don't matter nearly as much as the fact that you're saying them.

The moment a thought pops into your head that has the chance of causing her to feel attractive, desirable and kissable, just say it. Whenever you feel that twinge of gratitude for how she makes your life so much better in so many little ways, share the feeling with her right then and there, or better yet, pick up a blank greeting card and put your thoughts to paper. When you hear your buddies moan about their girl problems and you're struck with the profound sense of how lucky you are to have the woman you do, call her on your way home and tell her! Learn what it is that she prizes about herself– what she is truly proud of—whether it's her professional pursuits, personal attributes, or contributions to the good of others. Once you discover these areas, take every opportunity to recognize her and let her know that you are aware of what she does, that you appreciate how well she does it, and most importantly, that you truly get her for who she *really* is. This isn't complicated! Granted, it's not necessarily easy, either. It takes some time and energy to build self-awareness and channel that elusive sixth sense a man needs to fully get in tune with the woman he loves. Still, the recipe is very simple: Think it. Feel it. Say it. You don't have to be a master chef—just need enough trips to the kitchen to get the hang of it.

SELF-ESTEEM

In theory, self-esteem is a variable that is blind to gender, affecting men and women's desire for words of affirmation equally. Still, this one is so tricky—so precarious! Most of us struggle from time to time with our self-confidence. There is a natural ebb and flow of power in relationships, even long-term committed ones. At any given point in time, one partner may feel more vulnerable or invested than the other, only to see it reverse course as circumstances change. For some people, however, the problem descends deeper than situational dips in self-confidence; for them, it's a foundational deficit in self-love.

Low self-esteem in a romantic partner can create a type of double-edged sword when it comes to words of affirmation. If your significant other struggles with low self-esteem, your first thought might be to shower him or her with loving affirmations. It's a simple matter of metabolism, right? She isn't producing enough self-love, so the obvious solution is to keep feeding her words of love, day and night, until they finally take. But that's the issue; these words may never take! While it's true the approach above will work with some people who suffer from low self-esteem, the fact is many others struggle to believe the affirming messages they're being fed. The words can backfire completely, forcing the recipient to feel anxious. The intended meaning is therefore unable to penetrate the confusion and becomes entirely lost.

What can you do, then, if you're partnered with someone like this? First, you really need to *know* him—learn what makes him tick, what triggers him, what issues strike to the core of his self-esteem problem. You may discover that he gets triggered by some key things, but not others. You may learn that he does, indeed, have an appetite for words of affirmation in certain areas, just not those areas that spark internal conflict. For example, a man who was ridiculed as a child for being overweight and ugly might have a difficult time believing you when you tell him he "looks very handsome in his new suit." These misdirected words of affirmation might make him feel like he's being lied to, sending him once again to that dark place where he doubts himself and feels humiliated all over again. On the other hand, he may have no qualms when you tell your neighbors about his recent promotion at work, commenting on how "brilliant he is."

The only way to really know what will work is through compassionate dialogue and considerable trial and error. Be patient and keep plugging away to find the words of affirmation that hit the mark. If *you're* the one struggling with low self-esteem, you need to be equally patient. Do the best you can to trust the messages your partner sends you. Try to be an open book and give your partner valuable feedback about your thoughts, feelings and reactions. Most important, we suggest that you seek out professional, individual counseling that will help you get to the root causes of the problem and begin to transform the way you think about yourself. The internal work you do in therapy can do wonders for your relationship.

FAMILY CULTURE

Some of you have experienced this kind of social situation before. A friend invites you over for dinner and introduces you to his family. Everything seems to be normal for the first 10 minutes or so as you shake hands and exchange names, but soon things pick up where they left off before the doorbell rang. That's when the fun begins! You listen as the matriarch of the home scurries around the kitchen to get dinner ready, all the while complaining to her sister about how her youngest is 24 years old but *still living at home*. If that weren't awkward enough, he's standing in the kitchen listening to the whole thing! Then you hear what sounds like a fierce argument coming from the other room, but the tension is quickly broken by a round of raucous laughter. It turns out the brothers are amusing themselves by taking shots at one another, but the merciless way they exploit each other's personal failures and embarrassments makes you cringe. Then, just as things seem to quiet down for the moment, a disgruntled grandfather launches a barrage of profanity at a television news anchor talking about proposed changes in Medicare. At this point, it's all become just a little bit overwhelming. You hadn't expected culture shock as an appetizer!

So, was it an example of cruelty, or simply *culture*? Actually, the way you answer that will tell you a lot about the kind of family you grew up in. As we asked in our chapter on conflict (chapter five), was yours the kind of family that chose your words carefully—the "if you can't say nothin' nice" type of family? Were your parents quick to praise you for a job well done? Did they complement you for being "smart" or "talented?" If not, were they the regimented, principled type of family that didn't say much either way, descended from a tradition of old-school family culture in which love and acceptance was something that was more *assumed* than *said*? Or, perhaps, would you have been entirely at home with the family in our scenario above? If you're standing strong after an upbringing full of criticism, dark sarcasm, and ruthless teasing, then more power to you! Who's to say that didn't help you build character and some thick skin for what is sometimes a cruel world out there. Still, you should probably be careful when inviting friends over for dinner. They may not find your family culture so easy to digest.

The point here is that your current appetite for words of affirmation is likely affected by family culture. If, for example, you are from the second type of family above—the kind that really didn't affirm or need affirmation for much of anything—then you may have a metabolic mismatch with an only child who grew up consuming praise like popcorn at the movies. Such a couple could be a good match in so many other ways, but this need for verbal validation is dire enough for some people that an insufficient amount could lead to serious disappointment and eventual dissolution. An even worse mismatch would occur if you put this same praise-loving person with one of the brothers from our dinner family above. There might not be anything "eventual" about the dissolution of *that* relationship! In fact, it might not last beyond the first few "digs."

If you're in a relationship that struggles in this area, take the time to get to know your partner's family culture. Ask! Tell each other stories from childhood. Have fun with it! You need the background information in order to understand what's shaped your partner's communication patterns and appetite for words of affirmation. Understanding leads to patience and empathy, two virtues you'll want to lean on as you make the necessary adjustments in both what affirmations you send to your partner and what you expect in return. In the end it's all about finding the right degree of compromise. But that takes time and practice like anything else in love. Just keep communicating and let each other know when things get out of balance.

FOOD FOR THOUGHT: Jimmy Evans of "Marriage Today" noted three types of destructive family communication (NewLafayette.org, September 8, 2015):

1. Silent treatment (used to punish or avoid)
2. Verbal abuse (cursing, name-calling, and intimidation)
3. Verbal manipulation (dishonesty, half-truths, exploitation)

RELATIONSHIP-SPECIFIC DYNAMICS

Just when you think you know yourself, someone can come into your life and change everything! The reality is that our metabolic need for validation through words is not a static thing; it changes along with the people in our lives. As consistent as personality may be over the lifespan, our relationship dynamics change all the time, thus affecting our own wants and needs for affirming language from our romantic partners. Sometimes gradual, other times sudden, changes can occur when there is a significant gap between your need for words of affirmation and a new romantic partner's ability to provide them. For example, you may find that while past partners were generally able to meet your high standards, your new partner is unnervingly reserved and unexpressive. Needless to say, this can rock the love-metabolic boat.

Our need for words of affirmation not only changes with the arrival of a new relationship, they can also change within an existing relationship. Take, for instance, a couple that has been together for six years. In a weak moment, one succumbs to opportunity and cheats on the other with a younger, more attractive and fit co-worker. Almost certainly, the violated party will experience an increased need for affirming words in the aftermath of betrayal. The heart is never hungrier than when it's hurt, and it will no doubt require a steady diet of positive communication for this couple to survive. Whether they be sincere expressions of remorse for wrongs or gratitude for forgiveness received—whether they come in the form of compliments or spontaneous reassurances of love and appreciation—words of affirmation are never more important than when couples begin the painstaking journey of healing broken hearts and shattered trust.

Healing does not necessarily erase scars, however. Past wrongs can leave a lot of little speed bumps for a new lover to navigate. So it was with Barbara, who entered into a committed relationship with Steven several months ago. Divorced more than three years, she spent 10 long and lonely years doing her best to endure a marriage to a man who rarely, if ever, emerged from the black hole of his own depression. She was lucky to get an occasional compliment or encouraging word. No surprise, after a decade of feeling unnoticed, unvalued and unwanted, Barbara's appetite for words of affirmation changed dramatically. Desperate to avoid falling into a similar relational trap, she was barely aware of how this increased need for affirmation shaped and colored her perception of Steven's words and deeds.

On one occasion, Steven called Barbara on his way to her place, informing her that he had stopped into the grocery store to pick up some wine and snacks for their evening. A thoughtful move on his part, yes? It would appear so, but for Barbara, this considerate gesture was overshadowed by her sense that he showed absolutely no urgency—no raw desire—to beat the clock to be with her after a week apart. She had not expected this "unexpected" errand, and even though he was calling her in an obvious display of thoughtfulness, she interpreted his delay as *thoughtlessness*. What he said was, "Hi, honey. I thought I would stop by the store and see if there is anything I could pick up for you."

What she heard was, "Hi, honey, unfortunately a bottle of wine is more important than my time with you." What she really wanted and *needed* to hear was, "Hi, honey, I'm on my way to see you right now. It's been such a long week apart and I really miss you! In fact, I better slow down or I might get pulled over! I wondered, though, if I should stop really quick to pick up some wine for us or, better yet, if we could go together to get some later." Translation: You are *noticed*, *valued* and *wanted*, an underlying message of affirmation that stands in direct opposition to the one established by a disappointing decade of marital neglect.

As with Barbara, experiences we have in past relationships and current ones shape our desire for words of affirmation. If your story is similar to Barbara's, or if you endured the kind of infidelity mentioned in the first example above, then it is vitally important that you become mindful of the ebb and flow of thoughts and emotions that occur as you cautiously move forward in your current relationship. It is so easy to be triggered emotionally—to dredge up old unsavory feelings. Once you start feeling them, it is very difficult to avoid the pitfalls of distorted interpretation and irrational thinking, leaving you little chance to accurately decipher the true intentions behind your companion's words and actions. Emotional health and healing are not gained overnight, unfortunately, and you may need to seek professional counseling services to help you on your way.

Of course, having the self-awareness, courage, and skill to communicate your thoughts and feelings to your love-partner is critical. They deserve the chance to prove their metal! But they can't tailor their messages of affirmation to meet your needs if they don't understand your needs. This can be raw territory—a place where couples have to be willing to patiently and lovingly bleed with one another. But fair or not, distorted or not, your partner needs to know your perspective, even if the conversation is difficult to have.

Couple's Quiz: WORDS

Answer each question by rating the variable of F.I.D. using a number from the scale below. Then ask your partner to do the same. Later, you'll add the total scores to a worksheet in the concluding chapter.

> How satisfied are you with your partner's
> use of **AFFIRMING WORDS**?

For you . . .

SUBJECT	FREQUENCY	INTENSITY	DURATION	SCORE
Words				

For your partner . . .

SUBJECT	FREQUENCY	INTENSITY	DURATION	SCORE
Words				

Rating Scale
5 = very satisfied; **4** = satisfied; **3** = somewhat satisfied;
2 = somewhat dissatisfied; **1** = dissatisfied; **0** = very dissatisfied

Total Score Key
0–5 = Needs a lot of work; **6–10** = Needs some attention; **11–15** = Doing well

CHAPTER 10

Making Time for Quality Time

"Quality!" If ever there were a word whose meaning was steeped in subjectivity, this is it. As they say, one man's trash is another man's treasure. What constitutes quality, then, is entirely up for debate, and this certainly applies to time we spend with significant others. Just as our first couple, Jon and Jennifer, discovered the meaning and importance of "quality communication," some people may learn that what they need, more than anything, is for the time that they spend together to *really count*! What makes together-time add up to something meaningful is up to you and your partner. Take the time to learn one other's love-metabolic needs.

As we have shown so far in this book, identifying an unmet need—in this case, together-time—can only take you so far. True connection and intimacy are forged by deciphering the optimal balance of being together often enough, for the right amount of time, and with the right degree of focus and attention on one another (F.I.D.). An aging, retired couple, for instance, may spend almost every waking moment together, a fact that really says nothing at all about the quality of that time. They may sit and read, share tid-bits from the newspaper with each other, or work in the garden together. Is that enough? Surely, the "frequency" and "duration" components are more than sufficient; they are no doubt spending enough hours, days and weeks in each other's company. That leaves one all-important factor to consider: intensity! When this couple sits, reads, gardens, and shares news stories, are they truly *connecting*? Do they garner a sense of warmth, trust and understanding from their time, or are they barely present with one another as they play out the daily charade? Even if their routine works to meet the needs of one, chances are it might not fulfill the other.

Many couples, regardless of their station in life, fall into this predicament—the "high volume/low quality together-time" trap—often without even realizing that one or the other is feeling disconnected and unfulfilled. They know that they spend quite a bit of time together. They may come home consistently around the same time each day, walk the dog together, eat dinner, and watch their favorite TV dramas until bedtime. They may even have their own bedtime ritual. Add a couple of kids to the mix, and you likely have even more systematic, predictable "together" time: soccer practices, recitals, meals, homework help, and more elaborate bedtime rituals. By all appearances, these couples have all the together time they could possibly hope for. But then, there's the real question we're asking here: What does all this time do for a couple's relationship? Far too many couples, especially those with younger children, find their dedicated, quality together-time dwindle until they barely have any. The costs to their relationship are paid in such small amounts, over so much time, they often don't realize the damage.

FOOD FOR THOUGHT: On average, American men tend to find more "spare time" in their day than do women, but not by much. They spend an average of six hours per day engaging in leisure activities. Not far behind them are American women with 5.2 hours. Some of this leisure time is spent socializing, exercising, and pursuing hobbies, but none of these top the list. Can you guess what's number one? That's right,

TV-watching. While those surveyed said they valued spending time with partners, family, and friends the most, nearly three hours per day are spent in front of the tube (from "American Time Use Survey Summary," Bureau of Labor Statistics, June 24, 2015).

BILL AND LINDA: A CASE OF TOO LITTLE, TOO LATE

Bill could have sworn he had hatched the perfect plan to fix things! Realizing his wife was slowly drifting away and was in desperate need of more quality time, Bill decided to pull out all the stops and organize a sexy, romantic get-a-way to Las Vegas. But as we said before, the individual—not the couple—defines the meaning of "quality." Unfortunately for Bill, his definition of "quality" was a bit too loose for Linda. He subscribed to the idea that the quality of a vacation spent with his wife was determined by the types of exciting activities he could organize and how much money he could throw her way to keep her occupied. Linda could care less about all that. Her idea of a good time was *reconnecting* with her husband.

In spite of their differences, Bill managed to entice Linda to go to Vegas, not only with the promise of a great time together, but also with the added incentive of a full-day spa treatment *just for her!* Bill's offer was, in essence, an attempt to balance the scales after admitting that he had plans to indulge himself in one little poker tournament. As Linda found out shortly after arriving at the hotel, that "one little" poker tournament soon morphed into an exhaustive, time-sucking weekend event, while her "day-long" spa treatment turned out to be over within an *hour and a half!* Linda had lots of time on her hands; Bill's hands were filled with face cards. It wasn't a good situation. Disappointed and alone, Linda spent the bulk of her leisure time poolside texting her friends.

But Bill *did* promise a dinner and show later! Thank god for that, she thought, clinging to a small but fading hope that their "romantic getaway" might actually include something romantic. As she would soon discover, however, Bill returned too late, too inebriated, and too worn out from a day of gambling to think of anything else but crashing on their bed for the night. The next day brought more of the same, offering even less hope than the day before that he would rescue her from her disappointment. This little vacation of theirs was fast becoming a lost cause for Linda, as well as a sad reminder of the southward direction their relationship had been taking for some time.

Sensing something was likely amiss on this second day of his poker tournament, Bill strategically made a bold move by having flowers delivered to their room. He didn't even need to leave the casino floor to pull it off! Nice try, Bill, but completely the wrong love language. When Linda discovered the lovely bouquet of flowers, they could do very little—even with all their beauty and fragrance—to dispel the stench that had fully permeated their Las Vegas love nest. Nothing he did—no amount of money, gifts, or distractions—would work on her now. No, she needed one thing and one thing only—for him to quit that damn tournament and stick by her side for the rest of their miserable trip. By that point, it didn't matter to her if they spent the rest of their vacation ordering crappy room service; however it happened, she just needed to feel like she was more important than a pile of poker chips!

Sadly, that never happened. In the end, Linda went home feeling defeated, lonely, and more convinced than ever that her relationship with Bill was in real trouble. As for Bill, it is uncertain how he fared in the tournament. But whatever his earnings, it's doubtful his winnings outnumbered the points he lost with his wife. Even so, Bill appeared to be oblivious to the true extent of his losses, telling others upon their return that they had a "great trip to Vegas together." Needless to say, those same people received a much different report from Linda.

MARK AND KATE: A CASE OF TAKING TIME TO MAKE TIME

Mark, on the other hand, was a man who would not repeat Bill's mistakes as he contemplated the perfect romantic get-a-way with *his* wife, Kate. Already in tune with Kate's need for quality time and already keenly aware of how she defines "quality," he set out to plan a trip that would offer them the best of all worlds: a little something for him, a little something for her, and a whole lot of something for *them*. Unlike Bill, however, he actually included his wife in the planning, making sure they were clear about what they wanted out of the trip. Mark thought it might be fun to experience the fires of a Hawaiian volcano. Kate was going for something less dramatic and dangerous. She really wanted to enjoy the beauty and serenity of tropical gardens and experience Hawaiian wildlife, spending her time observing and learning about sea turtles.

With their individual interests declared and accounted for, the real magic happened when Mark and Kate consciously made sure to list activities they would both enjoy *together*—activities that placed primary importance on satisfying their need for quality time. To that end, they made plans to snorkel the best beaches in Kauai, a hobby they equally enjoyed. They even scheduled "down time," which included lazy afternoons at the pool, cocktail hours and lots of "intimate" time in their room. Yes, they actually took out their planners and scheduled all of this in, as if they were two professionals planning for an important business meeting. That's the value they put on their quality time together, a mutual understanding that only fully developed after years of patient communication and interpersonal discovery. They came home feeling more bonded, more secure, and more in love than before they left.

So, on which side of the world do you find your relationship? Flourishing in Hawaii or floundering in Vegas? If you're a woman, do you feel satisfied with the frequency, duration and intensity of the time you spend with your romantic partner, like Kate does? Or is your time together leaving you empty, as it does for Linda? If you're a man, do you feel like Bill, haphazardly trying to satisfy a partner's need for quality time but never quite figuring out what you're doing wrong? Or have you reached a place of relational maturity in which you truly understand your life partner's definition of (and appetite for) quality time, like Mark?

The key is in the communication. You have to take the time to talk about quality time and what it really means to your partner. What kind of love-metabolic rate are you dealing with? Does a little go a long way for her, or does she churn and burn, using up her quality time calories at break-neck speed? Does he still feel loved and connected, even though it's been three weeks since he has had any significant alone time with you? Get to know your significant other's appetite for quality time and then begin to plan for it from a love-metabolic point-of-view. Consider how often and how long you need to be together to meet the need. Most importantly, decide how engaged, immersed and focused you should be during that time. Like Mark and Kate, prize your time together! Schedule it in like you would an important medical appointment. Remove all the distractions—even kids—to make sure that it happens. This will help both of you come away feeling much like Mark and Kate did after their trip to Hawaii: More bonded, more secure, and more *in love*.

FOOD FOR THOUGHT: Taking time out to visit family is one of the top reasons that couple argue during their "romantic get-a-ways" (from the online travel blog, "Skycanner").

Couple's Quiz: QUALITY TIME

Answer each question by rating the variable of F.I.D. using a number from the scale below. Then ask your partner to do the same. Later, you'll add the total scores to a worksheet in the concluding chapter.

> How satisfied are you with the **QUALITY TIME** you get with your partner?

For you . . .

SUBJECT	FREQUENCY	INTENSITY	DURATION	SCORE
Quality Time				

For your partner . . .

SUBJECT	FREQUENCY	INTENSITY	DURATION	SCORE
Quality Time				

Rating Scale
5 = very satisfied; **4** = satisfied; **3** = somewhat satisfied;
2 = somewhat dissatisfied; **1** = dissatisfied; **0** = very dissatisfied

Total Score Key
0–5 = Needs a lot of work; **6–10** = Needs some attention; **11–15** = Doing well

CHAPTER 11

Getting the Gift Right

Who doesn't love getting a gift? It's safe to assume that most of us do. Still, as much as we *love* receiving them, receiving them doesn't always mean we feel *loved*. This fact is often lost on the gift-giver, particularly the *male* gift-giver. How many guys do you know who conveniently use this as the go-to "fix-all" when they mess up? Forget an anniversary = a dozen roses. Get upset and say hurtful things = gift certificate for a massage. And the list goes on. Men who do this are obviously missing the fundamental point that most women's brains aren't wired to "keep score." Making amends doesn't come down to a nice, tidy accounting process in which relational debits and credits balance each other out. It really comes down to how a woman *feels* when the dust of the apology cycle settles. Will she view his gift as a communication of love or merely an admission of guilt? Will she see his offering as a sincere gesture of reconciliation, or will she feel insulted and undervalued by his attempt to buy her off?

While the "man in the doghouse" may be a worn out stereotype, it effectively underscores the point that the power of a gift depends on the love-value the recipient places on it. That's a truth that applies equally to women *and* men. It's not so much a matter of what is felt in the *giving* as much as what is felt in the *receiving*. In other words, love sincerely communicated through a gift can easily get lost in translation if gift-giving isn't the recipient's love language. Assuming that receiving gifts is one of your partner's love languages, then the issue of love metabolism comes into play. Sure, you presented him with a gift that *you* really liked, but was it the right gift *for him,* at the right time, with the right underlying message? How hard did you really try? Did your gift represent a significant sacrifice on your part, if not of money then of time, energy, or creativity? Did your gift reflect how well you know the ins and outs of *who he is*? Getting this right will make the message unmistakably clear and insure that you illicit the kind of love-response you're hoping for.

YOU LOVE HER—YOU LOVE HER NOT

To our male readers: Let's say you are thinking about sending flowers as a routine way to your woman's heart. Let's also assume that receiving gifts is your would-be recipient's primary love language. Now it's a matter of getting all the love-metabolic variables lined up for maximum romantic effect! Here are the questions you should ask yourself:

1. How often should I send flowers? Find the right frequency to create the maximum love-effect, a task that requires some research on your part. Let's assume you've figured out that she likes to receive flowers often. She regards them as an essential expression of love. If you only send them a couple of times a year, then she probably feels like you don't love her enough. That may not be true for you, but remember, this is not only about speaking *her* language, it is also about speaking it often enough that she believes you. Now, let's say she's the kind of woman who feels that flowers should be reserved for special occasions and more profound declarations of love. In this case, sending flowers too often could cheapen the gesture and

dilute the intended message. Either way—whatever side of the spectrum she falls on—it's important to find that frequency sweet-spot for sending flowers, or any gift, for that matter.

2. When should I send flowers? You know that receiving flowers makes her feel loved. What you need to figure out is whether that feeling comes by way of satisfying expectations or by thrilling her with the unexpected! Simply put, should flowers be the product of planning or the result of passionate impulse? Is she the type of woman that would feel neglected without flowers on Valentine's Day or Mother's Day? If so, your work is laid out for you and all you need is the will, a few dollars, and a calendar. On the other hand, she might be the type of woman who basks in the thrill of spontaneity and the unexpected feeling of love it brings her. In that case, your very predictable Mother's Day bouquet might be seen as little more than an unimaginative move on your part to fulfill a romantic obligation. Many women enjoy a little of both: They like to count on flowers on certain special days, but they also love the occasional surprise.

3. What kind of flowers should I send? Flowers are flowers, right? Wrong. If life and relationships have taught you nothing, you should at least have learned that most women crave a man who knows their "favorite things" list, inside and out. Knowing her favorite perfume or favorite animal, for example, is not merely a matter of trivia; it is tantamount to really knowing *her*. And so it is with flowers. Get to know what her favorite flowers are. Chances are she has different favorites, depending on the season or circumstances. Different flowers probably say different things to her and it will pay dividends to learn them. If you do your homework and choose wisely, you'll craft a message that not only says, "I love you," but one that also says, "I get you." For many women, "I love you" and "I get you" are one in the same.

FOOD FOR THOUGHT: There are approximately 400,000 types of flowers in the world. Newsflash: Not all women prefer roses. Don't be fooled by all the marketing.

---

4. How should I send flowers? Sometimes you may not have a choice in the matter, but if you do, consider the method of delivery and how creative or personal you can make it. What would it mean to her if you were able to deliver them in person to her office, or if you placed them on the floor just inside the entry way so they were the first thing she noticed when she opened the front door? How would she feel to come home and see a trail of flower petals leading to a beautiful, full bouquet sitting on the dining table, surrounded by the warm glow of candles, a couple of glasses of wine, and dinner ready to serve? Remember: For many people, creativity communicates love.

5. Should I send a card, too? Depending on the occasion, the answer to this is most certainly "yes." A well-timed, heartfelt card can be the glue that sticks long after the flowers have faded. Still, you don't want to overdo it. In our chapter on communication (chapter three), we talked more about how to use the written word to satisfy love-metabolic needs. Assuming a card is called for, here's another question: What kind of card? Standard greeting card? Rare, designer card? Small? Large? Electronic? Well, that all depends on her tastes, doesn't it (back to the favorites list)? Ironically, you may find that a completely blank card might work best to reach your goal. You may not be a Pulitzer Prize winner, but the message you send will be uniquely yours and will undoubtedly mean the most to her. Crafting a message with your own pen signals thought and effort on your part, which in turn signals to her that she is worth all that thought and effort.

It all sounds simple enough—go to the store and pick up some flowers! Unfortunately, finding metabolic balance in a relationship is anything but simple, but as they say, sometimes the most difficult undertakings are the most rewarding. Certainly, there are few things more gratifying and sustaining than a loving romantic partnership! As complex as the process of interpersonal discovery may be, it's anything but complicated when you break it down into small, manageable pieces. Little things go a long way toward reaching the goal of love-metabolic balance, such as getting to know what's on your partner's "favorites list" and tailoring your gift-giving to match it. How hard is *that?* Simply ask questions. Better yet, quietly observe. Take the time to learn what your partner likes and pay close attention to his or her responses. If you get it right, you'll usually see the positive effects spill over into other areas of your relationship.

Don't be afraid to ask for feedback after giving a gift—when some time has passed and the moment is more appropriate. When you broach the subject, don't ask, "How did you like that crock-pot I got you," but rather ask a question that will unlock some insight into the value your partner placed on the gesture, itself: "So, did I get it right with that crock-pot I got you last month for your birthday? *I know you were talking about making stews that would last throughout the week.*" When you *receive* a gift from your romantic partner, don't be afraid to go beyond the obligatory responses, such as, "This is perfect," or, "I love it." Add that little extra to your words that gives your partner a chance to see inside: "This is perfect! *You must have noticed how much I've been eyeing this.*" Translation: You get me, you know me, and I appreciate you for it! Just a little extra communication on both the giving and receiving ends can make a tremendous difference.

GETTING THE GIFT RIGHT: A BIRTHDAY TO REMEMBER

Marshall hadn't made much of birthdays since he was a kid, but receiving gifts had been his primary love-language since his grandmother had planned the perfect neighborhood party for his sixth birthday. Even as an adult, a good gift still meant a lot to Marshall. Now, his wife, Patrice, didn't speak the language of gift-giving particularly well. While that may have been so, Patrice was also very emotionally aware. She had read *The Five Love Languages* and could see the disconnect. She wanted to learn how to speak Marshall's love language and figured his 45th birthday was the perfect time to do it.

Knowing his love of sports—and major league baseball in particular—she secretly purchased tickets to an upcoming match-up between the Seattle Mariners and his former hometown team, the Oakland Athletics. The only way she tipped her hand at all was to insist weeks in advance that he clear his schedule for the appointed Friday night. When the day came, she excitedly announced the agenda for their evening, telling him to fetch his A's cap and jersey while she readied her Mariner's gear. They arrived a good hour before the game, as planned. She wanted to make sure that he had plenty of time to take it all in. They spent that hour behind the left-center fence watching batting practice, munching on appetizers, and enjoying a few drinks. Before the first pitch was ever thrown, Marshall was already aware of how much time, attention, and love she had put into creating the perfect birthday gift.

Had it stopped there, it would have been enough for him to fully get the message, but to his surprise there was even more to come. In the middle of the seventh inning, Patrice nudged his shoulder and turned his attention to the massive scoreboard monitor, which suddenly flashed a personalized message: "Born an A's fan but slowly & surely becoming an M's fan. Happy 45th, Marshall!" He was blown away! How did she pull that off? How long had she planned this? The entire night, from top to bottom, had been all for *him*. For a man whose unrequited love language was gift-giving and receiving, Marshall felt an awful lot of love that night. In fact, that love inevitably lingered over the weeks and months that followed. For a woman who took the time to learn a different love language and speak it at the right time, in *just* the right way, Patrice felt pretty good, too. Yeah, she knew full well she had hit it out of the park!

ACTIVITY: MY FAVORITE 40

Test yourself to see how many of your partner's favorite 40 you know. Make it a fun date night activity. Which of you knows the other best? Game on!

1. Color
2. Holiday
3. Time of day (e.g., morning or night)
4. Family member/relative
5. Best friends (past and present)
6. Movie
7. TV show
8. Actor
9. Song
10. Band/artist
11. City (visited)
12. Country (visited)
13. Dream destination
14. School subject
15. School teacher
16. Sport (to play/watch)
17. Sports star
18. Professional/college teams
19. Perfume/cologne

20. Tree, plant, flower
21. Park
22. Beach
23. Recreational activity (e.g., hiking)
24. Meal
25. Dessert
26. Hot drink/cold drink
27. Alcoholic drink
28. Book/magazine
29. Author
30. Animal (in the wild)
31. Pet animal
32. Musical instrument
33. Physical feature (your own/others)
34. Character trait (your own/other)
35. Dream career
36. Dream purchase (boat, luxury car, cabin on the lake, etc.)
37. Charitable cause/organization
38. Dream living situation (high-rise condo, mansion in the suburbs, small cottage on acreage)
39. Architectural style
40. Historical figure

Couple's Quiz: GIFTS

Answer each question by rating the variable of F.I.D. using a number from the scale below. Then ask your partner to do the same. Later, you'll add the total scores to a worksheet in the concluding chapter.

How satisfied are you with your partner's **GIFT-GIVING?**

For you . . .

SUBJECT	FREQUENCY	INTENSITY	DURATION	SCORE
Gifts				

For your partner . . .

SUBJECT	FREQUENCY	INTENSITY	DURATION	SCORE
Gifts				

Rating Scale
5 = very satisfied; **4** = satisfied; **3** = somewhat satisfied;
2 = somewhat dissatisfied; **1** = dissatisfied; **0** = very dissatisfied

Total Score Key
0–5 = Needs a lot of work; **6–10** = Needs some attention; **11–15** = Doing well

CHAPTER 12

Acts of Service That Satisfy

Sadly, as noble as it is to serve another, service is not always received as a message of love. By definition, you would think service *is* love. Still, as with almost everything in our book, it comes down to perspective. Sometimes your acts of service aren't truly appreciated for what they are because your recipient doesn't see the act as a "service" to begin with. Instead, your recipient might view the act as the fulfillment of an obligation or expectation. Thus, if you're simply "doing your duty," then your gesture is anything but special. Let's face it: Completing a "routine task" has little chance to evoke special feelings of any kind, let alone *love*.

Much of your perspective develops early, formed by family culture and childhood experiences with key caregivers. Take Carmen, for example, who grew up in a home in which her father assumed the role of "fix-it man." He was always tinkering with this and that, taking things apart and putting them back together. If any appliance or gadget stopped working properly, no one in the house worried about it because dad would be all over it as soon as the problem was discovered. He was the handyman equivalent of Old Faithful—amazingly powerful and mind-numbingly reliable at the same time. Year after year, dad did his thing. The unfortunate result (from a love-language standpoint) was that her father's sacrifices on the family's behalf were seen as little more than fulfilling a duly-appointed role. In Carmen's world, that's *just what dads do*!

Fast forward decades later to Carmen's relationship with her husband, Hector. Hector's childhood home featured a father who often worked overtime to make ends meet and sometimes traveled out of state to score the best opportunities for his family. That meant that most repairs were left to those back home, namely his mother and two brothers. Hector remembers how frustrated his mother would become trying to fix or replace things that broke, but he also recalls how thrilled and appreciative she was when he and his brothers would solve the problem on their own. On such occasions, his mother's ecstatic outbursts filled their home with exclamations of gratitude and the loud smack of kisses on cheeks. There could be no mistaking that Hector's mom felt *loved* when this happened. They knew how to speak her love language and she openly rewarded them for it.

Do you see the disconnect here? Carmen and Hector are in different camps when it comes to interpreting acts of service. Their differences in perspective is particularly disconcerting for Hector, who has spent many hours of his spare time and energy over the years finding opportunities to express his love for Carmen through little acts of service. Thinking all the while that Carmen would eventually get the message of love if he just kept at it, he undertook various tasks he assumed would be both unexpected *and* appreciated. Whether he built new shelves for the kitchen cupboards, drove her car to the service station to fill a low tire, or got his tools out to fix some jewelry she hadn't been able to wear in some time, he tried his best to make an impact. Still, he came away with very little to show for his efforts.

Did Carmen truly not appreciate his efforts? Well, in a word, yes she did. She did thank him each time, after all. Still, to Hector her expressions of gratitude seemed hollow. The words just didn't pop the same way that his mother's *thank you*s did all those years ago. Nor did Carmen's facial expressions or body language come anywhere near the same level of crazy, euphoric appreciation. Then again, why should they? For Carmen, the matter was relatively simple. She failed to give Hector the excitement he craved because, in her mind, there was nothing to get excited *about*!

FOOD FOR THOUGHT: One of the largest and most used categories on the Angie's List Website is "Guide to Hiring a Handyman." You might want to make sure that acts of service is your partner's love language before you tackle a massive project.

Clearly, Carmen's experience with her family of origin shaped her perceptions and virtually assured that acts of service would take a back seat as a love language. The problem is that the back seat was where Hector was comfortable sitting, a place from which his declarations of love ultimately fell on deaf ears. But let's change the dynamics of the story. Let's suppose that acts of service were, indeed, Carmen's primary love language. That would certainly turn things around for Hector. Even so, there's still the matter of love metabolism—that intricate process of identifying the right acts of service, then executing them often enough, at the right times, with the right degree of care (F.I.D.). So assuming Carmen's love language is, indeed, acts of service, let's tackle a new scenario to illustrate the approach Hector might take to strike the right metabolic balance with his acts of service.

Carmen loves it when Hector takes care of her car. That means just about everything, from maintenance to repairs to cleaning. In the past she felt completely loved and taken care of, while recently she's only been mildly appreciative. Why the difference? Well, years ago Hector started taking over the maintenance duties for Carmen's vehicle, which included an occasional oil change. At first, he did the work himself. He'd go out to buy filters and replacement oil, spend a couple hours on labor, and get quite dirty in the process. Furthermore, he had to carve out the time to do it all. All this sent quite a message to Carmen, one that hit the mark.

Then, over time, he found it convenient to drop the car off for servicing while he completed other errands on his list. This soon became a routine, occurring every few months. What he gained in time, however, he lost in points with Carmen. Now, that may seem unreasonable that he should be judged for what most people would do anyway: Get their car serviced by professionals. But in truth she wasn't judging him. Carmen never blamed him for only doing what made sense. Then again, she couldn't really control how she felt about the change, either. So in the end, she was grateful for Hector's thoughtfulness but not feeling *so loved* by it.

It wasn't long before Hector noticed that Carmen's expressions of gratitude began to wane over time, and he began to wonder what had gone wrong. After thinking about it for some time, he realized what was missing. The extra effort was gone, and with it that extra message of love she so appreciated. He knew what he needed to do, but he had also become accustomed to the convenience and speed of the commercial oil change option. So he worked on a compromise that would recover the lost love language without costing him half of Saturday to do it.

That next Saturday morning, Hector took Carmen's vehicle according to plan. Carmen watched him pull out of the driveway, expecting nothing different. Nothing *was* different, in fact, until he pulled back into the driveway a few hours later with a bag full of car cleaning and detailing supplies. Without so much as setting foot in the house, Hector took out his new wash mitt, filled a bucket with soap and water, and started washing the outside of her car. Once sparkling clean, he grabbed the vacuum and went to work on the inside. After that, he wiped down every last inch of the interior with cleaner, followed by a conditioner that made the dash and seats shine like new! Carmen didn't realize what he had done for her until Monday morning, as she prepared to go to work. She was so moved by the surprise, she promptly went back into the house, threw her arms around Hector, and thanked him for making her car look and feel so amazing! Judging by the intensity of the hug, Hector could sense that she wasn't just talking about her car.

So what's the love-metabolic lesson to be learned? It's actually quite simple. Although it takes time, attention and patience, you will find ways to meet your partner's need for acts of service, just like Hector did. Just as he went that extra mile to take care of his wife's car, as well as her heart, you can learn to do the same. Keep communicating and fine-tuning. Eventually you'll find that elusive sweet spot so many couples hope to find—that place where *how often*, *how long*, and *how much* combine in just the right way to satisfy love-metabolic needs.

Couple's Quiz: SERVICE

Answer each question by rating the variable of F.I.D. using a number from the scale below. Then ask your partner to do the same. Later, you'll add the total scores to a worksheet in the concluding chapter.

How satisfied are you with your partner's **ACTS OF SERVICE?**

For you . . .

SUBJECT	FREQUENCY	INTENSITY	DURATION	SCORE
Service				

For your partner . . .

SUBJECT	FREQUENCY	INTENSITY	DURATION	SCORE
Service				

Rating Scale
5 = very satisfied; **4** = satisfied; **3** = somewhat satisfied;
2 = somewhat dissatisfied; **1** = dissatisfied; **0** = very dissatisfied

Total Score Key
0–5 = Needs a lot of work; **6–10** = Needs some attention; **11–15** = Doing well

CHAPTER 13

Hungry for Touch

Clearly, this will be a sensitive topic. You can get dizzy thinking about all the variables that go into satisfying a romantic partner's need for touch. Just when you think you have it figured out, you find the very same thing that worked on your partner three times before backfires on the fourth. You may be even more confused when you give your partner exactly the kind of physical affection he told you he liked, only to feel him pull away in embarrassment. It's complicated! It takes patience and communication to navigate, for sure, but like everything else we've considered in this book, the rewards are worth it.

At the outset, let's go ahead and break down "touch" into two main categories, just as they are in the book, *The Five Love Languages*. First is "implicit touch." This kind of physical affection can be subtle and even subconscious. Sometimes it feels so natural and instinctive that it requires about as much thought as breathing. Implicit touch includes hand-holding, kissing (non-erotic), hugging, snuggling, caressing, tickling, massaging (non-erotic), and even sitting close. "Explicit touch," on the other hand, may be as instinctive as the implicit category, but it involves that spirit of Eros that has been responsible for the human race becoming as enormous as it is. Explicit touch is characterized by passionate, erotic impulses and triggers that wonderful cocktail of neurotransmitters that makes us feel so good and keeps us coming back for more. Speaking of coming back for more, we'll give explicit touch its proper due in our chapter on *love metabolism and sex.* For now, we'll focus on implicit touch.

Whether you're talking about implicit or explicit touch, you can't assume that any given form of physical affection is good for your love-partner, as natural and instinctive as it may be to you and others you know. Even with touch, it comes down to love languages and love metabolism. Is it his primary or secondary love language? If so, great—assuming you also prefer touch. Once you know he likes it, needs it, and *feels love* from it, then it's a matter of F.I.D. How should you touch him? Where should you touch him? For how long? How intensely? Now, it may sound like we're getting into sexual foreplay territory, but these questions apply equally to non-sexual types of touching, as well.

Consider this scenario: A man you've only been dating a few weeks (or even a few years if you're like some couples) invites you to his place to watch a football game on TV. Shortly after you arrive—after the greetings, hugs, and kisses are over with and all the action in the room is confined to a couch, a bowl of chips, a remote control, and a flat screen—you reach over to touch him lightly on the hand. He fails to respond. He doesn't jerk his hand away, so that's good. He doesn't slowly slide it out from under yours to grab more corn chips, so that's good, too. The problem is he doesn't move it at all. It's not bad; it's not good. It's nothing—but that doesn't really help you learn anything about him, at least not at first.

About 10 minutes later, you feel a small caress on your finger. His hand actually responds! Well, at least one finger responds, but you'll take it. He removes his hand for a moment to grab the remote, makes an adjustment on the volume, and sets it down. Understandable. But then he doesn't return his hand to yours, which is now resting all alone on his knee where he left it. You instinctively wiggle your hand around to signal that it's *still* there . . . waiting . . . exposed . . . cold . . . lonely. He watches his game. You wiggle even more. He watches his game. You go for broke and actually relocate your hand an inch or so, caressing his knee in the process. *He watches his game.*

You finally come to the decision to stop fussing over it, and just as you're about to retreat back to your side of the couch, his hand returns to take yours. But this time he adds something more as he slips one of his fingers in between yours. You're pleasantly surprised, especially considering that you had just given up hope that your little game could compete with the one on TV. Then it hits you: The game's not on right now. It's a commercial break! Hmmmm. You think back to when he responded earlier—that moment when he caressed your hand with his finger. You realize that was during a commercial break, too.

Is this a pattern, you wonder? It might be too early to tell, but you are determined to find out. You hatch a little experiment. As soon as the football game returns to the screen, you are the one to pull away first, paying close attention to any non-verbal cues that tell you he's aware of what's happened. In characteristic fashion, he gives absolutely none. In fact, the only movement he makes is to reach for the chips and turn up the volume—*again*. Instead of taking it personally, you channel your inner scientist and focus instead on completing your experiment. You're actually starting to have fun with this! The next commercial break can't arrive fast enough. That's when you'll unveil the next step in your plan, a move that couldn't be easier to make as it requires, well, absolutely nothing.

The break in the action finally comes and this time, you keep your hands completely to yourself. Now the waiting game begins. Will he notice? Will *he* be the one to make a move? Does he even want to hold my hand in the first place? Just then, you see him grab the remote, turn down the volume, and glance at you for a brief second as if in a kind of senseless daze. A split-second later his eyes instinctively shift down toward your hand, as if to say, "Oh, yeah . . . hand . . . yes . . . I remember." Then he reaches for it, just as you thought—or rather hoped he might!

He even gives your clasped hands a little pat with his free hand, as if to say, "There . . . all back to normal!" At that point he smiles and starts up a conversation, and you realize that you now understand something about his taste for touch that you didn't know before. While there is still much more experimenting to do before you can definitively determine when, where, and how much he likes to be touched, you at least have this scientific conclusion in the books: His appetite for touch decreases when his favorite team is playing football, while his appetite for corn chips remains stable.

Let's suppose you've been dating him now for six months. You know so much more about him than you did on that football Sunday. Your little foray into the scientific method that day has inspired you to keep going with your analysis, so much so that you're actually keeping a journal to record any and all details you discover about his needs and preferences for touch. Here is a snapshot of some of what you've recorded:

July 3rd: Spent the day hiking and picnicking. Talked about growing up and that his parents didn't really show much affection, especially in public. Held hands quite a bit, but noticed he would break away when other hikers passed. Trail got pretty busy. Finally no one around—he grabbed my hand and pulled me over behind a tree. Great kiss while it lasted! He soon got nervous that someone might see—kept looking around.

July 14th: Went out for a night on the town. Had some drinks, dinner. Walked around a lot afterward in the cool air. Great romantic energy! Loved it! He got very snuggly/touchy—more than ever, even with other couples walking by. Pointed out later that he seemed really affectionate. Asked why he didn't seem self-conscious. He wasn't sure. Thought maybe it had to do with loosening up a little with drinks. Also being on a "date," and the vibe of the city at night. Said he noticed other couples around. Just felt more natural—like the right time and place to let loose a little.

July 22nd: Attended a funeral together. Didn't touch me at all the entire time. Reached over to caress his arm during the service—no reciprocation, no glance, nothing.

August 5th: Spent evening together after he shared that he got a bad review at work. Tried to cheer him up—hugged him and rubbed his back—no response physically. No initiation on his part. Hugged me back when I left but didn't feel sincere. Confused. Thought he really needed comfort but apparently not.

August 6th: Talked on the phone for an hour. Asked him for help understanding the mixed messages—sometimes likes it when we touch, sometimes doesn't. Figured out what happened at the funeral. Said he was so glad I was there to support him. Told him it didn't seem that way. Asked him why he was so physically distant. He had to think for a while about it but talked through it with me. Said funerals remind him of churches, which remind him of his grandmother. Spent many Sundays with grandma—pretty strict and proper woman—all about presentation. Never showed affection in front of others at church. Never held grandpa's hand that he can remember. Asked him about what happened last night. Finally got out of him that he's not good with being touched when he feels bad about himself . . . like he doesn't deserve it. Told me that just being there helped a lot and that the hug at the end felt nice. Go figure.

August 10th: Realizing that we never seem to hold a hug long enough for me. He's always the one to break away first. Need to pay more attention to this. Tempted to feel like maybe I care more about him than he does me.

August 12th: During a hug just came out and asked him if he would mind holding me a little longer. Said OK. Felt great. He even squeezed a little more this time. Felt safe and loved. Talked after about it. He asked if he was "doing it wrong" or something. Told him that I just like long hugs better. Said he's OK with that but that longer hugs get awkward for him—doesn't know what to do with himself. He likes hugs for sure but also likes to get them over with. Ha! Gotta work on a compromise here.

FOOD FOR THOUGHT: For the average adult, the skin has a surface area between 16.1 to 21.5 square feet and is filled with nerve endings. That gives you plenty of opportunity for skin-to-skin connection!

And so your journal goes from there. Can you see all the interpersonal discovery going on here? You have accomplished so much already. After six short months, you understand so many of the ins and outs—all those little love-metabolic variables that help ensure that you're both getting the most out of implicit physical touch. You know something about his family culture around physical affection and some childhood experiences that still influence him. You've learned how his moods affect his desire for touch. You've discerned the answer to what otherwise is a paradox: Public displays of affection are usually a bad idea, unless, of course, you're out on the town on a cool, romantic night. More than anything, you have begun the all-important process of compromise. He needs you to back off in certain settings and you're adjusting. You need longer hugs to get that love juju going and *he's* adjusting. That's what this book is all about—learning and compromising until you discover the best ways to satisfy one another's hunger for love.

Couple's Quiz: **TOUCH**

Answer each question by rating the variable of F.I.D. using a number from the scale below. Then ask your partner to do the same. Later, you'll add the total scores to a worksheet in the concluding chapter.

How satisfied are you with your partner's **PHYSICAL AFFECTION?**

For you . . .

SUBJECT	FREQUENCY	INTENSITY	DURATION	SCORE
Touch				

For your partner . . .

SUBJECT	FREQUENCY	INTENSITY	DURATION	SCORE
Touch				

Rating Scale
5 = very satisfied; **4** = satisfied; **3** = somewhat satisfied;
2 = somewhat dissatisfied; **1** = dissatisfied; **0** = very dissatisfied

Total Score Key
0–5 = Needs a lot of work; **6–10** = Needs some attention; **11–15** = Doing well

CHAPTER 14

The Love-Language Buffet Called Valentine's Day

Perhaps there is no better day of the year to illustrate all that can go right—and all that can go woefully wrong—than Valentine's Day. It's a day full of love-metabolic hits and misses—a time when expectations are high and appetites are even higher. We're not simply referring to hunger for chocolate, here. We are talking about a hyper-focused need for receiving the right love-language—in just the right way. We all like to feel loved and cherished, especially by the one that is most special to us. But for many star-struck lovers, that desire gets a caffeine boost every February. Make no mistake, this is a fabulous opportunity to take your relationship to new heights! On the other hand, it's a day when you could just as easily crash and burn. Our hope is to illustrate, in precise detail, the kinds of romantic moves that will help you avoid such a fate.

Below is a list of the five love languages, followed by some of the great—and not-so-great—creative Valentine's ideas that we have encountered over the years. Remember, as good as an idea may sound to you, you won't hit the target unless first you use the right love language, and second, you use it in such a way that your romantic partner feels satisfied. If you haven't learned much about your partner's "favorite list" up to this point in time, work quickly. February can be very sneaky, appearing all too soon after a very busy holiday season of gift-giving. As you will readily see, most of these creative expressions of love are designed to point Cupid's arrow at the *female* heart. Then again, is that really a surprise to anyone? Let's face it, Valentine's Day is a day for *men* to get the metabolic balance right. Whatever happens in return is a bonus. Guys, the pressure is on!

FOOD FOR THOUGHT: Men spend twice as much money on Valentine's Day as women do. Men spend an average of $108, while women average $53. Americans collectively spend $18.6 billion each Valentine's Day (CNN Money Report by Annalyn Kurtz, February 14, 2013).

WORDS OF AFFIRMATION: DOS

1. Call her and leave a message on her cell phone first thing in the morning, wishing her a happy Valentine's Day. This lets her know that she is the first thing on your mind and that you're in control of the day. There are big points to be scored, here! Depending on your personality (and your relationship dynamics), you may want to stretch your limits and share some deeper feelings you have for her—things you wouldn't ordinarily say. You might tell her the "top three things" you love most about her. *Another list?* Yes, another list. You could also share some memories of times when she made *you* feel loved. Perhaps you're daring enough to spice up your message with some "sexy talk." Go ahead. Get a little edgy and flirt with her. Tease her. Tell her you're tied up in knots thinking about how good she's going to look later in that new cocktail dress. Give her a hint about your plans for the evening and tell her that she's going to be very "busy." You get the picture. Be daring—but also be yourself.

2. After several hours have passed, follow the phone call with a customized "e-card." There are many online greeting card services

that are either free or inexpensive to join. Once you have found the online card that best captures the moment, you'll want to customize it as much as possible. This is usually very simple and often involves typing in a personal message that will be displayed after the animation has concluded. This is where a couple of sentences from your own heart and mind can make all the difference. After the creative work is done, surprise her by having the e-card automatically delivered to her email address.

3. With two digital forms of verbal affection under your belt, it's now time to "give her something she can feel!" Arrange it so that she receives a tangible, paper greeting card at the end of her day. Whether you buy it or create it, make sure it reflects the love, passion and desire you feel for her. If you do buy a card, you might want to add heart-felt words of your own; they will undoubtedly mean the most to her. If you strike the right cord, don't be surprised if your words pop up again 20 years down the road in a drawer somewhere. Whether inside drawers or hearts, women keep these things close.

4. Create a type of advent calendar with Valentine's cards. For example, you might create or purchase seven cards and arrange things so that she opens one each day, with the last one—and best one—saved for Valentine's Day itself. You might even go a step further and "hide" each card in such a way that she stumbles upon them during her daily routine. Start day one with a simple message that gets the sparks going. Each day after that, you'll fan the flames a little more until Valentine's Day, when you'll unveil your most personal, powerful message yet.

5. Depending on your artistic skills and talents (or your immunity to embarrassment), try writing her a poem. If you're so inclined, recite it to her in person. Channel you inner Don Juan and set the whole thing to music and candle light. She'll be overcome as you pour her a glass of her favorite wine, lead her by the hand to the sofa—music

and candles already going—and begin to share your love through poetic verse. If poetry just isn't your thing, write her a song instead. Sing it to her. If your voice would do more damage than good to the relationship, write an instrumental and play it for her. Perhaps your words are better expressed through your artwork, such as a sketch, portrait or painting. Pour your feelings on to the canvas and allow her to interpret what it means to *her*. Of course, if you can't sing, play or paint, you can always just pop in a CD of a carefully selected song that captures exactly how you feel about her. Something as simple as that can be extremely effective.

6. Tell the world you love her through social media! Yes, love has come of age—a digital age in which *"I love you"* is often said with an iPhone. Cyberspace socializing may not be your thing at all, but on this one, special day, you might reevaluate your aversion to cyber-babble. Bite the bullet by posting a message on Facebook, Twitter or Instagram that proves you're proud to be with her and not afraid to show it. It really doesn't matter how many people "like" it or "comment" on it. All that matters is how she feels after you post it.

WORDS OF AFFIRMATION: DO NOTS

1. DO NOT select a humorous greeting card. Please don't misunderstand: Joking and laughing are appropriate—and even important—in building healthy relationships. But this is NOT the day for that! Sure, many women say they love a man who can make them laugh, but all the side-splitting one-liners in the world will never reach her heart like pure words of love and desire. Not on February 14th, they won't.

2. DO NOT say things like, "I'll pay for the five course dinner if you'll serve me a little 'dessert' when we get home tonight ..." Never make her feel that she owes you a debt for your efforts, especially one that should be repaid through sexual favors. No, don't go there. She's so much more than that to you, so don't cheapen your message

with words that suggest you're expecting something in return. In fact, you *shouldn't* expect anything in return. As we said, if you get anything at all on Valentine's Day, consider it a bonus.

3. If dinner *is* in your plans, DO NOT allow her to pay for any portion of it, in spite of societal trends. Let chivalry make a comeback for one night!

4. DO NOT have her do any of the legwork to organize the date. *You* make the calls for reservations, tickets and babysitters.

GIFTS: DOS

1. Let her eat . . . chocolate! Let's first acknowledge that not all chocolate is equal. As with almost anything you may give her on Valentine's Day, your gifts send a resounding message. If you hand her a bag of waxy, discount chocolates from the grocery store, you're essentially saying, "My feelings for you are only as deep as the wax on these cherry cordials." If, on the other hand, you put your knowledge of her "favorites list" to good use and drive clear across town to get a box of her very favorite gourmet truffles, you're essentially saying, "I don't care about the distance or cost, I care only about *you*." Don't know her favorite kind of chocolate? Rest assured she has one, even if it hasn't come up yet. Don't be afraid to ask. Better yet, go as a couple to a quality candy shop sometime before Valentine's Day and take your time sampling various chocolate concoctions. It shouldn't be difficult to tell which ones resonate with her.

FOOD FOR THOUGHT: Good, pure chocolate is packed with resveratrol, which boosts levels of serotonin, the "feel good" neurochemical in the brain. So there's a good reason why some women say they "crave" chocolate (Dianna Walcutt, Ph.D., at PsychCentral. com, April, 2004)

---

2. Pamper, pamper, pamper! Try three different ways to give her the royal treatment on *her* special day:

   - Option 1—Treat her to an entire day at the spa. If that's too pricey for your budget, schedule a half-day or even an hour or two. This may include facials, body wraps, foot and hand rubs, and steam baths.
   - Option 2—Take her to get a massage on Valentine's Day. To make things more intriguing, sign up for a "couples" massage. You might even kick things up a notch by enclosing a gift certificate for additional sessions inside a greeting card.
   - Option 3—Take time off from work (big points here), take her to lunch, treat her to a manicure and pedicure, and finish it all off with happy hour drinks and dancing. "Wow" her even more by secretly picking out her outfit for the evening before you leave, perhaps a cocktail dress and a pair of shoes that will show off her gorgeous new toenails!

3. Referring to her "favorites list" once again, pick out or create several gifts you can easily hide all around your home. You may have to do some low-level stalking to ensure that you are familiar with all the places she would normally look (bathroom drawer, microwave, refrigerator, shower, bed, purse, car seat, etc.). You don't want her to miss anything, after all! You might even find a clever way to attach one word or phrase to each gift. Once she collects all of your gifts, she can decipher the correct word-order and arrive at a complete and very personal Valentine's message! Remember that a gift you make by hand can be just as effective—if not more effective—than a gift you purchase. This isn't about money. Plenty of wealthy men throw their cash around on Valentine's Day, to little effect. What matters is the message attached to your gift. Does it tell her you put in a lot of thought, time and effort? Does it say you *really* know her? The most expensive bottle of perfume means very little if she can't stand the scent.

4. Thrill her with flowers! OK, admittedly this may elicit less a thrill than a sense of relief that you came through as expected. We discussed this *ad nauseam* earlier. Still, there are a few curve balls you might throw to keep her off balance, such as delivering flowers to her office or placing a bouquet on the kitchen table so they are the first thing she sees before breakfast. Whether or not she is expecting flowers, make sure you pick up her favorites. Don't assume red roses are appropriate. In many cases they are, but you better know that going in. Otherwise, she may regard your offering as impersonal and uninspired. If you do settle on roses because they *are*, indeed, what she prefers on this special occasion, personalize the gesture by selecting one rose for each year you've been together. You might even assign each year a different rose color and work out a narrative that describes how each color represents some unique quality or trait she possesses. Do this one right and she'll melt faster than a box of cherry cordials on a hot car seat!

5. Adorn her with jewelry! Like red roses, though, jewelry can be every bit as impersonal as that autographed Taylor Swift poster you bought at the mall for your daughter. Expensive is not necessarily better, either. It all comes back to the message this piece of jewelry sends. Is it a ring that features her favorite type of metal? Is it a necklace with her favorite gem as the centerpiece? Is it a bracelet charm that reminds her of the place you met? You get the picture. You can impress her even more if you find or create jewelry with matching, his-and-her pieces. This could be something on the extravagant side, such as a pair of designer watches, or something more modest and homegrown, such as a pair of leather bracelets with both your names engraved on each. Certainly, the pieces you select should match each other *and* your style.

GIFTS: DO NOTS

1. DO NOT buy her lingerie—*on your own*. If you do, you run the risk of purchasing something she would never pick out herself. The last time we checked, lingerie isn't one size-fits-all, either. Again, what message are you trying to send in the first place? What you view as a sexy gift for *her* might easily be misconstrued as sexy gift for *you*. Don't make the same mistake so many would-be Romeos make each year on Valentine's Day, when their lovers get the sense that the entire day was nothing more than a self-serving charade designed to gratify the male sexual urge. Now, this is not to say that lingerie is not an appropriate gift. Far from it: Lingerie can generate all the sparks you hoped it could. You simply need to include her in the shopping! Plan it as a pre-Valentine's date and visit several stores to get ideas. Let her call the shots and lead you where she will. When she is comfortable enough to ask for feedback on something, be sure not to say, "Ooooh, that's hot!" Rather, choose your words more strategically; say something like, "Hmmmm . . . I would love to see you in *that*!" The all-important fact to remember here is that no woman wants to feel overshadowed by a piece of fabric. She wants to know that you desire her *without* it, as much as you do *with* it. It's all about feeling sexy as a person. The better she feels about herself before she puts on a piece of lingerie for the first time, the better it will feel for you when she *takes it off* for the first time.

2. There's nothing quite like a Valentine's gift that says, "You're special—now cook something for me!" *Please*, DO NOT buy her a kitchen appliance! Sure, on other occasions a toaster, crock-pot, or juicer might be the perfect gift, BUT NOT TODAY! You should know that Valentine's Day is meant to quench her thirst for love, not satisfy your hunger for waffles.

3. DO NOT make Valentine's Day "a day the entire family can enjoy!" Love and desire may be what created your kids, but don't expect your kids to ever return the favor. Kids are killers—romance killers,

to be precise. As we pointed out in the chapter on quality time, a couple can be so consumed with their family that they entirely forsake their partnership. Don't miss this opportunity for some much-needed romantic rejuvenation. Stop being parents for one night and try to remember what it was like to be lovers! You may need your own parents' help to pull it off, but whatever arrangements are necessary to take the kids off your hands for the night will be more than worth it.

4. If you happen to receive a Valentine's gift yourself, DO NOT devalue or discount her expression of love by saying, "You shouldn't have done this," or "This must have cost a lot of money." You may genuinely like the gift, but comments like these mask your gratitude. Accept her gift with a thank you and a kiss. Try to remember that questioning the gift is the same as questioning the message behind it.

QUALITY TIME: DOS

1. Treat her to a nice dinner out! As cliché as this may be—and it is—it doesn't get old if it's done correctly. There are as many ways to tantalize the pallet as there are to numb it. The same could be said for wooing women. The goal, then, is to create an evening that accomplishes both successfully: Delighting the taste buds while kindling the flame of romance. What is her favorite dish again, you ask? Do your homework. We have given you the "favorites list" form, for heaven's sake. Sit down together and start to *learn her*! As we mentioned before, you might not have to spend an inordinate amount of money on dinner to prove yourself. Ignore price, location, and reputation. Just focus on what works for *her*.

2. Take her on a long drive to a romantic destination. Plan stops along the way at sites, stores and cafes that you know she would really enjoy. One gentleman we know did just that and really "took his relationship to new heights!" He planned a snow day in the

mountains, capped with a private, evening gondola ride to a restaurant on one of the peaks. Sure, it sounds like a story-book day, but truth be told, it ended up being every bit as woeful as it was "woo-ful." He and his partner laugh now as they look back on getting stuck in a broken-down gondola and enduring a few other minor misfortunes. As it stands now, what she remembers are the sacrifices he made to give her the perfect day, while the memories of frostbitten limbs have all but faded.

3. Cook as fancy a dinner as you can manage! This one is easy—or hard—depending on your culinary capabilities. On the one hand, it's not complicated or difficult to plan. On the other, there are lots of ways to mess up the taste of food. A relaxing, romantic evening at home may be just what she needs, depending on how hectic her daily life is. If she spends a lot of time at home already, especially in the kitchen, this is probably not your best option. You want to make sure the experience is special for her, which usually means it's not something she experiences often.

FOOD FOR THOUGHT: According to AOL.Travel, two vacation spots you might want to avoid on Valentine's Day are 1. Dubai, where you can be arrested for kissing in public, and 2. Disneyland, where lines of screaming kids can kill the mood ("World's 7 Least Romantic Spots to Avoid on Valentine's Day" by Anna Brones, February 14, 2014).

QUALITY TIME: DO NOTS

1. DO NOT procrastinate! It's difficult to make quality time on Valentine's Day if you didn't spend some quality time ensuring you could actually get reservations for her favorite restaurant. Make sure you see February 14th coming! Call ahead and make those reservations early.

2. On this occasion, it's really a bad idea to allow the usual distractions to get in the way. Your main culprits: Car stereos and cell phones. When you're driving to your destination DO NOT fumble around trying to find songs you like. Even worse, DO NOT listen to a game broadcast, unless she is as big a sports fan as you are. Some women already feel like their men have more passion for their fantasy football roster than they do for *them*. When you arrive, DO NOT have your cell phone out. Don't check texts, answer voice-mails, or even check the Internet to look up things you happen to be talking about. Try to make her feel she's so compelling you can't take your eyes off her.

ACTS OF SERVICE: DOS

1. Chose a mundane task she doesn't enjoy and surprise her by having it done before she gets home. As we illustrated in the chapter on acts of service, it's important that you do something for her on Valentine's Day that she wouldn't ordinarily expect you to do. With that in mind, do whatever you think she will appreciate most.

2. Take some things that she does all the time off of her plate, such as getting breakfast ready or taking the kids to the bus stop. You might even spend the whole day with your kids so she can enjoy a restful day doing something she really wants to do for herself.

3. Again, cancel your other obligations if you can so you can focus on serving her. This will go incredibly far in proving that you're serious about her special day.

ACTS OF SERVICE: DO NOTS

There is really only one piece of advice that comes to mind, here. DO NOT plan to do things for her that in reality benefit "the household," such as cleaning out the attic or fixing a broken appliance. Don't misunderstand: These are definitely examples of acts of service, but they don't offer the kind of personalized pop you want on Valentine's Day.

PHYSICAL TOUCH: DOS

1. Touch a lot and often on Valentine's Day. This goes not only for "explicit touch," which is the kind that often comes to mind on this holiday for lovers, but also for "implicit" touch. If you go out to dinner, for example, she may like it more if you sat next to her, rather than across from her. Gently place your hand on her back when you open doors for her. Hold her hand when you're walking places.
2. Take a bath together. Kiss longer than usual. Give her a foot or back rub. You can figure out the rest of your night from there. Suffice it to say, it's important to show more physical affection on Valentine's Day.

PHYSICAL TOUCH: DO NOTS

1. DO NOT go overboard with touching. You have to know her love-metabolic limits for touch, especially in public. Be sensitive. You don't want to embarrass her or make her uncomfortable in any way.
2. DO NOT slather your skin with cologne, lotions, or other chemicals that you ordinarily wouldn't wear. DO NOT forget to brush your teeth or bring mints along. On a night when she craves closeness, don't make the goal difficult to accomplish.
3. For couples that live under the same roof, DO NOT—and we mean DO NOT—offer all the kinds of affection we've mentioned to this point, only to kiss her goodnight, leave the room, and finish your day with some TV and microwave popcorn. For some women, this

would mark disaster. The *Titanic* also showed its guests the time of their lives, but we all know how *that* story ended. Avoid the iceberg. Stay close to her for the rest of the night.

PART III

CHAPTER 15

Sex That Sizzles

Warning: We're about to turn up the heat in the kitchen! It's time to talk about sex—the ultimate case-in-point for all things love metabolism. Can you think of anything that's more subject to the ebb and flow of appetites and tolerance levels than sex? You want a little; you want a lot. You like it some of the time; you like it most of the time. You like it planned and predictable; you like it spontaneous and passionate. You probably prefer one or the other, right? But here's the thing about sex—things can change! The moon hangs at just the right angle, a warm wind blows off the water in just the right way, and suddenly your lover's embrace hits you like it never has before. That's when you know the rest of the night will be anything but ordinary. But then, that's the beautiful thing about sex. It has the ability to defy your expectations, challenge your thinking, and take you to new heights of pleasure, intimacy and happiness.

Happiness? That's right—we said it. Can sex really make you happy? Can it improve your overall sense of well-being? Of course, you already know sex can be a real rush in the moment—the biochemical equivalent of the most intense thrill ride you've ever dared to experience! But did you know studies conclusively reveal that the greatest benefits of sex—or, to be more specific, of *good* sex—continue long after the "ride has come to a complete and full stop"? The secret can be summed up in one word: Oxytocin. Part neurotransmitter, part hormone, oxytocin is the biochemical invitation to relax and stay a while. Affectionately named the "cuddle chemical" by some, its effect on bonding and intimacy lingers long after its flash-in-the-pan chemical cousin, dopamine, has concluded its firework show. Dopamine is the "lusty attraction chemical" that gets people (even strangers) together in the first place. While sex is often considered the ultimate dopamine rush—and it truly is—it's actually the oxytocin that creates that coveted "closeness." Put another way, dopamine makes *love*, while oxytocin makes *lovers*. No surprise, committed couples who are also committed "lovers" get a healthy dose of both; they enjoy making love and they do it often, which gives them plenty of dopamine highs and, more importantly, lots of good oxytocin bonding for the long-haul.

So what does all this biochemical-babble mean? Rather than indulge in a further discussion on biochemistry, let's just go straight to the results. Couples who have healthy, active sex lives feel more safe and committed. They cheat less than other couples. *Go figure.* They enjoy increased self-esteem, reduced stress, and better focus at work. The positive effects aren't merely emotional, either; good sex also invites good physical health. Ever heard that age-old excuse, "not tonight . . . I have a headache?" You might want to think twice before using *that one* again. Good sex can actually help to relieve headache pain! And the list goes on from there. People in committed, sexually active relationships can improve the quality of their sleep, build muscle tone, improve their cardiovascular health, lower their blood pressure, and even live longer than couples that just aren't getting it!

So we've made our case: Sex is really, really good for you. But the real question to consider from here is what constitutes "good" sex. As with everything in this book, the answer depends on many personal preference and experiential factors. It's not simply a matter of giving sex a pass or fail grade. There are reasons why some sex is good for you and some is not, and chances are those reasons have to do with the right combination of frequency, intensity and duration.

With that in mind, let's break down F.I.D.'s relationship with sex and talk about the profound effect each component has on your level of sexual desire and satisfaction.

FOOD FOR THOUGHT: How much sex are married couples having? According to a study printed in the University of Chicago Press, married couples average seven times per month. That's a little less than twice a week (from an article entitled, "How Often Do Normal Couples Have Sex?," from www.everydayfamily.com)

SEX AND FREQUENCY

"Oh yeah, we do it a lot," answers a woman in a couples counseling session. "I don't know what he's complaining about." Her husband, sitting next to her with his arms folded, responds sarcastically, "A lot? So once—maybe twice—a week if I'm *really* lucky is your idea of 'a lot'?" Sound dicey? Sure, you could say it is, but this kind of snarky dialogue is unfortunately a very common occurrence in session. In the case above, they actually agree on the frequency numbers, which isn't a given for other couples. Like the average married couple, they have sex on average one to two times per week. Now, you might think that's pretty good!

Certainly, this woman does, but her husband has an entirely different idea about what defines "a lot of sex." And that, quite frankly, underscores the entire point here, namely that the definition of "lots of sex" is entirely subject to a person's love metabolism.

To further complicate issues, your appetite for sex is anything but static. Unless you are a walking, talking sex hormone with only one thing on your mind, you are like the rest of us whose appetites for sexual contact wax and wane.

There are many possible reasons why love-metabolic needs for sex fluctuate. Some reasons are situational, meaning that desire is affected by changing circumstances. Sometimes, changes in physical health can affect appetite—or even ability—for sexual activity. At other times, the factors that shape desire for sex are neither physical nor situational in nature, but instead spring from attitudes or beliefs passed down through family or religious culture. In some tragic cases, desire is seriously compromised due to past sexual trauma. Whatever the reason, it's vitally important that you take the time to explore the factors that alternately increase or decrease your own desire for sex, and then begin to explore your partner's. We'll help you start that conversation by offering up some common factors that affect the frequency of sex.

The Newness of a Relationship

New relationship = high frequency. Bet on it! You've probably heard that old saying that goes something like this:

Put a penny in a jar for every time you have sex with your spouse during the first year of marriage and take one out for every time you have sex from year two forward; 20 years later (or some untold number of years in the future) you'll finally empty the pennies from the jar.

However the saying *actually* goes, it does somewhat accurately tell the story of many couples' sex lives. If you're new to each other, chances are good you're getting a lot of sex. We won't concern ourselves with the quality of that sex, at this point. We'll get more into that when we consider the intensity variable of F.I.D. Suffice it to say, while your ability to effectively please one another usually increases through the years, the number of attempts often decreases over time, at least for many couples. It's a very sad truth indeed, but this doesn't have to be the case!

The fact is, many couples do sustain the frequency well after the novelty of a new relationship wears off and the period of "discovery" has passed. As much as possible, they fall asleep together each night. They make sacrifices in their schedules and actively plan to be together—to put themselves in positions that allow for intimacy. For example, couples with young kids routinely schedule babysitting. This allows them to relax for a while, get back in touch again with how it feels to be a couple, and get into the mood for some quality—albeit quiet—intimate contact when they get home. If they want to let loose more, then they have the babysitter stay the night while they grab a nearby hotel. Other couples unencumbered by the demands of children ensure they get some one-on-one time by actually scheduling it, as though making an important business appointment.

Now, we realize this idea might kill the spirit of reckless spontaneity that often gives sex a real spark, but let's be realistic. Can you really just leave it all to chance? How many times have you come home, exhausted from all you've done, thrown something in the microwave, and burned your last reserves of energy eating a Hot Pockets® sandwich and watching back-to-back sitcoms? You might have been excited at the thought of sex with your partner earlier in the day, but by 10 p.m. you had no choice but to throw in the towel. So you go to sleep with a brain buzzing with blue screen glare when, instead, you could have been basking in nature's neuro-chemical afterglow. That's really not a good trade by anyone's standards.

But that's life, isn't it? That's why you have to grab it by the horns to stay horny! Start using your planner. Come to think of it, use your smart phone, too. Shoot your partner a text invitation or reminder of your romantic plans for the evening and make sure to add some creative, sexy emoticons if it suits your personality. Even if it doesn't, try it anyway and shake things up. One man we know found it completely foreign to send smiley faces, thinking the practice juvenile and pointless. What's more, he was worried that his new romantic interest would see his use of emoticons as a sign of laziness on his part—that he would rather just send a picture of a heart with an arrow through it than actually think of something clever to say. The truth, as he would discover, could not have been more conveniently ironic. It turns out she actually preferred sexy, lovey-dovey emoticons over words. Once he let that sink into his business-minded brain, he quickly recognized the amazing return on investment and in short order became an emoticon expert.

Perhaps he also realized another subtle fact: Supplying a little extra sweetness adds some of the unexpected to what's *already* expected. In that spirit, keep surprising your partner. Try to get home early before you begin your night of fun and frolic, preparing the room with fresh sheets and scented candles. The more you can do to prepare beforehand, the easier it will be to focus on enjoying one another when the moment arrives. Whatever you do, just make sure you schedule in time to enjoy sex with your partner. Oh, and don't be late for the meeting, either. You don't want to get fired!

Other Situational Factors

Even when you're doing just about everything you can to clear the way for love, things come up and life happens. Sometimes they are little things and at other times, they can be whopping game-changers, such as the arrival of a baby. As much joy as a newborn can bring, it usually means a lot of time, attention and sleep loss for one or both of you. The entire unrelenting, exhausting care-giving process is nature's way of telling you to stop doing the thing that got you into this mess in the first place. Naturally, the frequency of sex takes a nose-dive with a new baby in the house. On the other extreme, sometimes a death in the family is what interferes with an active sex life. Grief can easily overpower libido and just about every other life force, leaving you little to give your romantic partner. It's not always major life events that get in the way, however. Sometimes it's all the little stressors that add up to affect the desire for regular sex. Whether it's late hours at work, deadlines, travel, challenging kids, or even something as trivial as a messy house, life has a way of throwing lovers off balance.

Physical Factors

Disclaimer: We are about to refer to a sitcom to help illustrate our point for this next section. Please don't misconstrue this as a license to choose television over sex! We are well aware of how TV-watching and a healthy sex-life are in an epic battle with one another. Anyway, in an episode of the classic comedy series, *Everybody Loves Raymond*, Ray's wife, Debra, has suddenly become more sexually desirous and Ray doesn't have a clue as to why. Not that he's complaining, or anything, but still, he wonders about it. Putting the pieces together, he realizes that she's most primed for sex after her new workout class. Too curious and insecure for his own good, Ray attends her aerobics class and, to his dismay, finds a very attractive male instructor leading the group. You can guess how things fall apart from there. He manages to mess the class up, embarrass his wife, and lead them headlong into a discussion about the security of their marriage. That's when she offers up the kicker (and makes our point): The real reason she feels so hot and bothered after her workouts has nothing to do with the instructor, but rather the fact that she feels more confident, fit and attractive than usual.

And so it goes with real couples in the real world! Being in good shape pays dividends for sexual frequency, not to mention its positive effects on sexual performance and stamina. If you're physically fit, chances are very good that you're interested in having sex more often. Sometimes, though, it's not so much your actual fitness level as it is the psychological effect of "getting into shape" that increases desire. It feels good to improve our bodies—to get healthier and have more energy. The endorphins kick in and we start feeling better at a biochemical level. The recipe is pretty simple: When we start loving our own body more, we start craving our partner's body more (assuming he or she isn't heading in the opposite direction physically). We don't have to be supermodels or shrink back to our high school weight. The mere process of physical improvement is often aphrodisiac enough.

FOOD FOR THOUGHT: When a woman does cheat on her husband by having a one-night-stand, it tends to be with someone who is more physically fit than her husband (from "Lust, Love, and Loyalty," MSNBC iVillage Survey).

On the flip side, being physically unfit can definitely decrease libido, downgrade performance, and limit the frequency of sexual interaction. Sometimes it's not a matter of fitness at all. Some couples have limited opportunities for sex because of disease or chronic medical conditions. Other couples are affected by more foreseeable physiological changes, such as menopause in women and declining testosterone in men (or "MANopause" as some are now affectionately calling it). Other times the culprit isn't age or disease, but rather the medication that goes with it. There are plenty of pharmaceuticals out there that mess with the ability to achieve erections, lower libido, and restrict the ability to feel pleasure. If you're beset with any of these distractions to a healthy sex life, openly talk with your physician about it. Your pride shouldn't be bigger than your desire for lots of good sex! Whatever the condition, disease or medication, there might be solutions you either haven't tried or aren't aware of to help you get back your desire and ability for sex.

Religious and Family Culture

Ultimately, we're all individuals with our own love metabolism; we all desire sex differently. That said, values, attitudes and beliefs transmitted to us through generations can go a long way toward shaping that desire. Our intent here is not to engage in an argument that either disparages or elevates religion. We make no judgment about the validity or merits of religious teachings on the subject of sex. We will say, however, that whatever messages about human sexuality are intended by various faith traditions, some people interpret these messages in such a way that makes sexual intimacy difficult to even pursue, let alone to achieve.

This goes for males and females alike, although it certainly seems to affect women more than men. We have heard more than one story of women who—because of a lifetime of internalizing the feeling that sex before marriage was unnatural, perverse or even abominable—had great difficulties "flipping the switch" on their wedding night. Whatever their church leaders or its holy books *actually* taught about sex is beside the point. Distorted or not, their interpretation of that teaching and *how that interpretation made them feel* were all that mattered.

Think about it. If a girl spends her entire single life paranoid about sex and spends inordinate amounts of energy avoiding anything associated with it, it's simply not reasonable to expect that such ingrained fear would instantly vanish with the words, "I do!" This kind of deepseated anxiety isn't so easy to eradicate. Now, let's suppose this same girl adopted a less sinister outlook on sex. Let's say she was exposed to the same messaging as before, but instead internalized it this way:

Sex is actually a very good—even holy—thing to be cherished and enjoyed, but only within the bonds of marriage. It's OK to have these feelings. It's OK to desire sex. I simply have to wait for the right time.

In this case, she has received the message, taken ownership of the interpretation, and construed it positively. In so doing, she's effectively removed the psychological blocks to pleasure and fulfillment and is much more emotionally ready to enjoy sex when the moment finally arrives. This freedom of mind will also propel her to find satisfying ways to express her budding sexuality after she's married. Finally—and to our point—she's likely to want a whole lot more sex than before! Psychological blocks removed = greater pleasure = higher frequency!

While a healthy attitude toward sex is a deeply personal matter and each of us is ultimately responsible for the way we perceive and pursue our own sexual desires, the truth is many people are still hampered by unhealthy thinking in this regard. If you find that you or your partner are still trapped in the emotional fallout from years of fear, have the courage to share your feelings with one another. Tell your story. If you don't, for all you know your partner will go on thinking you're just boring in bed, or worse, that you simply aren't interested in sex. Don't let the good feelings of love freeze up like your sex-life. Talk it through, plant the seeds of understanding, and begin the compassionate move toward more fulfilling sex—one step at a time, one night at a time. If you're really stuck, you might consider seeking professional counseling from a licensed couple's therapist or, better yet, a pastoral counselor who truly understands how distorted beliefs can inhibit physical intimacy.

Moving away from religion now, sometimes the amount of sex you expect is shaped more by the example of your parents. Did your father and mother show affection to one another? Remember, this isn't a matter of right or wrong. It's an issue of family culture. Did you ever spy your dad stealing a kiss from mom in the kitchen, or did you ever catch him red-handed giving her a little "love pinch" from behind in the hallway? Do you remember evenings when you and your other siblings were conspicuously set up in the family room with a movie, game or some other distraction that would last for a couple hours, only to find that mom and dad's door was locked when you ventured away to find where they went? Yeah, your parents knew what they were doing! If this describes your family, it's likely you have assimilated a familiarity and comfort with sexual expression. Chances are also good that one or both of your parents talked openly with you about sex when the time was right. In short, the topic of sexual intimacy and expression are likely far from foreign or unsettling to you. On the contrary, sex, both in theory and practice, would probably feel quite free and natural.

If, on the other hand, your parents rarely, if ever, showed affection—if they treated each other with professional distance, as if they were merely principals in a family/business partnership, then it's reasonable to think that your attitudes toward sexual expression might be fairly restricted. We're not being deterministic, here, only discussing how family culture "may" affect frequency of sex. You may be one of those people who vowed to escape the frigidity of family culture and go for broke with your romantic partner. Again, it ultimately comes down to the individual. Still, the trappings of family culture can be very difficult to remove from the unconscious memory banks, especially if that culture not only ignored parental intimacy but also emitted messages that stifled future sexual expression.

Did your mother ever say things like, "Boys can't be trusted; they only want one thing"? Did your father ever guilt you before going out for the evening, telling you you're "dressed like a slut" and adding that "no self-respecting boy would ever be interested in you"? We hope your parents didn't say things like this. If they did, the feelings these messages evoked might be lurking somewhere in your psyche, affecting both your opinions about sexual openness and your appetite for sex. If this is you—and you're matched with someone who is oriented to a more playful, spontaneous and transparent show of sexual expression—you may be feeling quite uncomfortable. Needless to say, this could really affect how often you have sex with your romantic partner. As we said before, start the conversation with your partner and seek professional counseling if needed.

A Word About Sexual Trauma

Few things can negatively affect the desire for and frequency of sex more than sexually related trauma. We often assume that women are the primary targets, but the truth is that far too many men have experienced rape, incest and other childhood abuse that impact their desire and performance in the bedroom. We won't go into detail, as this subject extends beyond the scope of our book. But suffice it to say, past sexual abuse can completely stifle sexual intimacy. If you have been afflicted with sexual trauma, we strongly recommend you seek professional, individual counseling. Depending on your situation, you might also consider going with your partner to see a certified sex therapy specialist.

FOOD FOR THOUGHT: Don't worry, be happy! Happy couples have at least three times more sex per month than unhappy couples (from a study by M. Gary Neuman in Business Insider, March 6, 2015, businessinsider.com).

SEX AND INTENSITY

Candace was completely satisfied with how often she and Lucas made love. They almost always had sex on weekend nights and even sprinkled in some "afternoon delight" here and there. During the work-week, they managed at least one or two attempts. While Candace couldn't really ask for more sex, she was hoping for *better* sex. Quite honestly, she just wasn't feeling very stimulated. Sure, she would orgasm—not every time, but when she did it felt pretty good. Still, she couldn't help but compare their norm to the few times when her orgasms with Lucas were over-the-top. Something had happened on those occasions. She just wasn't sure what it was, nor was she certain how to replicate it. Was she in a more sensual mood—more relaxed? Was it the way he was touching her? Was it the fact that he had spent a lot of time gently caressing her back before sex, or did it have anything to do with the unusually consistent and sustained rhythm during intercourse? Whatever the case, it was simply too embarrassing to bring up with Lucas. She not only worried how she would sound, she was worried it would hurt his feelings. She didn't want him to feel that he was incapable of fully satisfying her.

Truth be told, he really *wasn't* satisfying her, but this sexual metabolic misfire wasn't entirely Lucas' fault. As a couple, they had never really summoned the courage—nor taken the time—to actually talk about satisfying each other in bed. They simply left things to fate. In Candace's case, she wasn't entirely confident that she understood her own body and sexual preferences, let alone how to communicate those preferences to Lucas. As for Lucas, he just did his thing each time, whatever that happened to be. He did his best to keep in tune with her responses and adapt accordingly, but then again, he could only go on what he was hearing in her voice, seeing on her face, and feeling in her movements. Thus, if she indicated signs of pleasure with a particular move, he was inclined to keep doing it. It didn't really enter his mind that she could be getting so much more out of the experience if he only did a little more of this, a little less of that, and a whole lot more of things he'd never thought of before.

So, what was the result of all this for Candace? *All the mediocre sex a woman could want!* Over time, though, Candace wanted better. After one particularly lack-luster encounter in the bedroom, she felt compelled to start researching ways to improve the quality of their sex life. That's when she came across the practice of sensate focus. In a nutshell, it's a method that couples use to explore one another's bodies, discover erogenous zones, and communicate likes and dislikes. Filled with hope and a tinge of erotic excitement, she decided then and there to plan a "sensate" date-night with Lucas.

When the night finally arrived, she made it clear to Lucas that this would not be "sex as usual." In fact, there wouldn't be any sex, at all. The end goal was not orgasm, it was discovery. They enjoyed a nice dinner, lit several candles in the bedroom, and then sat on the bed face to face, ready to begin their journey of touch. Candace led the way, touching, caressing, and rubbing Lucas' body, going area by area. She started with his feet, experimenting with varying speeds, levels of pressure, and parts of her hands and fingers. After each exercise, she stopped and asked him to respond. Surprised by how good "non-genital" touching could feel, Lucas gave her valuable feedback. When Lucas' turn came to do the experimenting, Candace was more than ready. He took his time and enjoyed the experience much more than she ever expected he would.

By the end of the evening, she and Lucas had a veritable treasure-trove of information about ways to arouse one another. In fact, Candace was so worked up by the end of her session, she found herself craving more. Kudos to Lucas, though, who gently reminded her of the original intention to keep things from going "there." She ultimately agreed and relented, but they didn't waste any time the next evening taking what they had learned and following things to their natural, climactic con-clusion. What was truly interesting about their sex that next evening is that the spirit of open communication hadn't ceased with the activities of their date night. Even in the thick of things, they found themselves keenly in tune with each other, asking questions and seeking feedback. As a result, Lucas was able to make adjustments that made intercourse much more pleasurable for Candace. Of course, they didn't perfect everything in one night, but Candace did experience another of those elusive, long-awaited big Os.

It was a sign of things to come. With time, patience and practice, Can-dace and Lucas were able to build an entire cache of skills that enhanced and intensified their sexual experience together. With that in mind, here is a snapshot of the variety of ways Candace and Lucas learned to plea-sure one another over time (placed into convenient categories):

1. Soft and Slow—This technique is characterized by the very gentle caressing that Candace was missing. She learned that she was especially sensitive on her back and that she preferred Lucas to use a light, sweeping motion with the palm of his hand. This very simple form of TLC was integral to reaching a state of relaxation, piquing her desire, and preparing her mind and body for greater states of arousal.

2. Tease and Tickle—Both Lucas and Candace found this one quite intriguing. Each one would take turns lightly running their fingertips up and down the other's legs, moving closer and closer with each sweep to the genital area. Just before arriving there, they would change course, starting the process over again from the shoulder. Eventually the ticking would give way to the "teasing" of more direct genital stimulation.

3. Strong and Tight—This was used when stimulation ramped up and they felt the urge to embrace. Candace, in particular, learned that once she reached a certain level of arousal, she really craved to be held tightly, with the gently caressing giving way to heavy stroking and passionate kissing.

4. Stop and Start—They used this powerful "stair-stepping" technique to greatly peak sensitivity and intensify their orgasms. Just before reaching climax, they would break the rhythm long enough to bring arousal levels only slightly down. Several moments later, they would resume the previous rhythm, repeating the process several times.

5. Rhythm and Rhyme—As the capstone strategy to intensify their experience down the stretch toward orgasm, they discovered a combination that really worked: consistent rhythm of movement mixed with consistent verbal communication. Some might call the latter "dirty talk," but for them it didn't really take that form. Just verbalizing the pleasure that each was feeling in the moment was enough to take their experience to new heights.

SEX AND DURATION

Sometimes sex falls short of being good because it simply doesn't last long enough. Now, you may be thinking that women are the ones getting the short end of the stick here. Not so fast. The fact is that men, too, are settling for less when sex is short-lived. How? For the reasons we just mentioned in the "stop and start" description, men can experience a more powerful climax by going longer, especially if they go just to the edge of orgasm several times before finally letting go. Obviously, going longer is good for the girl, too. It's well known that women prefer a prolonged sexual experience, mainly because their road of arousal from intrigue to intercourse to climax is typically much longer than a man's. That's not to say that a woman can't enjoy a heated moment of spontaneous passion in the kitchen or sneak off into the woods for some mischief. There's a time and place for everything in life, as they say, and that's no different for the various types of sex—from the "quickie" to the "all-nighters." The rule of thumb, though, is women take longer to get excited than men. The more excited they get, the more likely they are to enjoy the journey. The more they enjoy the journey, the more likely they are to experience more sustained and intense orgasms.

For some women, though, orgasm is a destination they rarely, if ever, reach. There can be various reasons for this problem. As mentioned before, sometimes irrational fears or other psychological blocks are at play. In other cases, a man's physical limitations are the issue (e.g., premature ejaculation, erectile dysfunction, etc.). If either side of the coin is affecting your relationship, you may find it helpful to consult with a licensed sex therapist. Quite often, though, a woman's failure to reach orgasm simply comes down to a man's lack of knowledge, patience and skills and a woman's failure to communicate her likes and dislikes.

Let's start with men. First and foremost, a man needs to realize the benefits of prolonged foreplay and intercourse for his female partner (and for him, too). There are many, in fact. If, for example, he engages in longer foreplay, that in turn cranks up her desire and progressively intensifies her pleasure. Her arousal, in turn, gets communicated back to him through her facial expressions, sighs and other physical responses. In turn, all of that gets him more excited as he realizes how much pleasure he is giving her, and so on. The entire experience becomes more intensified, enjoyable and memorable. Memorable sex usually increases desire for more good sex. It's a complete win for both partners!

Now, that doesn't mean that just because a man understands the value of longer sex he knows what to do with the extra time. That's where the woman comes in. Some women simply aren't comfortable teaching and coaching, especially in the moment. There are myriad overarching cultural and historical ramifications to consider when talking about the reasons why many women are stifled when it comes to the subject of sex. Wherever those reasons come from, it's high time for women to find their voice in the bedroom. Ladies, there is nothing wrong with telling your lover what feels good to you. There's no shame in ensuring that you get just as much out of the experience as he does. Remember, if it's good for you, it's ultimately good for him.

FOOD FOR THOUGHT: Among the factors that determine whether or not a woman feels satisfied with the sex, romance and passion in her marriage, the quality of the couple's friendship tops the list, accounting for 70%. And for men? Also 70% driven by friendship! Perhaps we're not on different planets, after all! (*The 7 Principles for Making Marriage Work*, John Gottman, Ph.D., Harmony Books 1999).

Communication around this issue can be tricky, but it really doesn't have to be if you engender the patience, trust and willingness that good lovers possess. If you trust your heart with him, then trust that he would want to do anything he could to create an optimal sexual experience for both of you. With a little courage and some forethought about what you might say before you frolic in bed the next time, you can start to give him the critical feedback he needs. As described in the sensate focus date-night example, perhaps you need him to spend a lot more time tickling and caressing, or maybe you need more extreme forms of stair-stepping, breaking away from intercourse for longer intervals and slowing things down dramatically (engaging in some slow-paced, sensual kissing, for example). Whatever the case, start the dialogue so you can have the good sex you deserve, the kind of long-lasting sex that produces lots of pleasurable orgasms, increased bonding and connection, and all the benefits to your health and well-being we mentioned earlier.

FOOD FOR THOUGHT: We fully recognize that longer-lasting sex may be the last thing on your mind. You're not always going to have the time, energy or patience for a gourmet, four-course experience, nor should you. As we said earlier, everything has a time and season. Just as you don't eat at the same sit-down restaurant every time you go out for dinner, your love-metabolic needs, tastes and preferences for sex can change. Everyone grabs fast food from time to time.

Couple's Quiz: **SEX**

Answer each question by rating the variable of F.I.D. using a number from the scale below. Then ask your partner to do the same. Later, you'll add the total scores to a worksheet in the concluding chapter.

How satisfied are you with your **SEX LIFE**?

For you . . .

SUBJECT	FREQUENCY	INTENSITY	DURATION	SCORE
Sex				

For your partner . . .

SUBJECT	FREQUENCY	INTENSITY	DURATION	SCORE
Sex				

Rating Scale
5 = very satisfied; **4** = satisfied; **3** = somewhat satisfied;
2 = somewhat dissatisfied; **1** = dissatisfied; **0** = very dissatisfied

Total Score Key
0–5 = Needs a lot of work; **6–10** = Needs some attention; **11–15** = Doing well

CHAPTER 16

Fitness for Two

You've seen it before, perhaps at a high school reunion or by random chance in a supermarket. You run into a couple you knew years earlier, but things have really changed. One looks young, while the other looks old. One is fit, spry, and radiant, while the other is heavy, sluggish, and run-down. Sadly, this is an accurate description of many couples. Sure, some take the slide into physical "unfitness" together, so at least their misery has company. But for many couples, divergent love-metabolic needs for physical activity lead to very different fitness destinations, and sometimes they find themselves on opposite ends of a substantial, almost irreconcilable divide.

Love-metabolic disparity with fitness can be a real problem for couples of any age, especially for those reaching mid-life and beyond. After all, one of the greatest benefits of having a romantic partner is having a companion for life's journey. Step by step, milestone by milestone, it's comforting to know someone is at your side, experiencing each stretch, climb and descent. Let's face it, though, it's not much fun when you're "over the hill" and one of you can't even make it up the hill to your house. If one slips into physical convalescence three times faster than the other, how can there *not* be issues between you? To be clear, we are not merely talking about physical appearance. Wrinkles happen. Bodies change. It's unavoidable. We are talking about lifestyle choices that affect the quality of a couple's connection.

That's what happened for Ken and Maria. Their love-metabolic needs for fitness and exercise were heading in opposite directions, and it was getting to be a real problem for Maria. It wasn't always that way, however. Ken was fairly fit throughout his 30s and 40s. He jogged every other day, hit the weight room at least twice a week, and didn't eat much junk food. As with many men that age, his body weight fluctuated, especially around the holidays. Still, he always seemed to return rather quickly to his set point range of plus or minus three pounds. While Maria certainly appreciated how much more physically attractive he was back then, what she remembers and longs for most was how they were so much more active together. They routinely took long Sunday evening walks, got up early for Saturday morning hikes (some of which were quite rigorous), and played competitively in an amateur tennis league.

See, for Maria and *her* love metabolism, being physically active together wasn't simply a matter of health and fitness. She hungered for it because physical activity largely defined who they were as a couple! It was a way of life. It was inextricably wrapped up in her entire sense of self and integral to the foundation of her relationship with Ken. True, she didn't always want to exercise together. She had plenty of dance and aerobic classes she enjoyed on her own, but pursuit of individual fitness goals only offered so many rewards. When she exercised with Ken, she not only reaped the physical and mental health benefits, but she also felt more connected, appreciated and validated. Validated? Yes, even that. That's because when Maria took to a trail and conquered it or set out to reach her personal best time in a 5K race, she felt more alive than ever. When he was there sweating with her every step of the way, he was seeing her at her best—witnessing, acknowledging, and embracing her truest self.

That's why it was so devastating for Maria when, in his late 40s, Ken tore up his knee in a softball tournament. It wasn't the injury itself or even the amount of time needed to recover from surgery that was difficult for her to take. She really felt for him and was quick to understand how discouraging this was for Ken, too. The real problem was that this setback marked the beginning of a love-metabolic shift in Ken, a decline in appetite for physical activity of any kind, let alone physical activity *with her.*

It certainly didn't happen overnight, though. At first he talked about the injury in positive terms, as though it were an opportunity for growth or a test of wills. Then, week by week, his determination to keep active, along with his plan to be extra careful to eat lean, healthy foods, diminished until he became quite content to sit in front of the TV with a bag of extra-butter microwave popcorn in his lap. Comments such as, "Can't wait to swim laps tonight" slowly gave way to "My knee's giving me fits, so why don't you go on ahead." Maria's patience and compassion didn't erode overnight, either. She understood his limitations and truly sympathized with his pain, but she couldn't ignore his gradual descent into fitness oblivion. She remembered how they sat down one evening and brainstormed all the activities he *could* engage in—many of which they could do together—that didn't involve putting pressure on the ligaments in his knee. In spite of how excited he was at first to give all these activities a try, she was now watching that excitement slowly fade with each passing week, every poor meal choice, and every pound gained.

In just over a year's time, Ken had morphed into a shadow of his former, fit self. He was 35 pounds heavier (that's right, 35, not 3.5), for starters. Needless to say, this affected his energy levels and desire to exercise, which by then had been reduced to occasional walks and trips to the driving range to hit golf balls. He felt less motivation in other areas, as well, including in the bedroom. In addition to his libido, his overall mood and sense of well-being also took a hit. In short, his vitality had been zapped and the loss had permeated almost every part of life. For

Maria, it was an even greater loss. Yes, she still loved him. True, she was still committed to the relationship. But she would be lying if she said her feelings hadn't changed. How could they not? One of the most treasured aspects of her relationship with Ken had faded, which in turn left her feeling abandoned. Whatever the reasons and wherever faults may lie, she was now pursuing a "life-path" all on her own, when she used to enjoy that path with a wonderful "life-path partner." It was, in a way, almost like grieving a death, of sorts. She still had Ken, the man, but she lost Ken, the complete partner. And with that, she lost a big piece of herself, too.

FOOD FOR THOUGHT: Sometimes we see some couples grow distant because one or the other's devotion to some form of physical exercise (e.g., long-distance cycling) effectively drives him or her outside the relationship to find people with a shared passion. This can become a problem if that passion consumes an excessive amount of time and one partner simply can't or won't participate. At the very least, it takes precious time away from the relationship and can lead to disinterest, disrespect and, in extreme cases, dissolution—all the more reason to find forms of fitness you like to do together!

It's true. Love-metabolic mismatches in fitness can really hurt relationships over time. Again, it's often a very slow kill, a gradual drift that seems harmless enough at first. Eventually, though, the tide of complacency can carry some partners so far out to sea that there's little hope of a return to healthy shores. Think about it! Do you really want to be with someone who just lets himself go—who seems more than content to slowly degenerate? The grim reaper can wait. You don't want to be with someone that holds you back or slows you down. You'd rather spend your time with someone that make you feel alive!

It's OK to feel this way. It's OK to want this from your partner. It's OK to ask for change. This is one of those love-metabolic issues where it's not so much a matter of personal tastes and preferences. Exercise is good for individuals; it's even better for couples—period! If you're the more-fit partner and are frustrated with the imbalance in your relationship, we can comfortably say that while it's important to compromise—even gives things up—when attempting to meet your partner's love-metabolic needs in general, this is not an area where less is more. The surgeon general, heaps of data, and common sense are on your side. If you're still looking for more to support your point of view, we can tell you that in our practices we have seen how exercise not only boosts an individual's emotional health and well-being, but how it creates happier, more fulfilled couples. It's a fact.

Now, if you're the more physically "unfit" partner, rise to the challenge and take the steps necessary to match your partner's fitness level. Assuming your partner isn't some kind of hell-bent, fitness freak, it shouldn't be such a daunting prospect. Yes, they'll have to show some patience and make some accommodations if they truly want to exercise "with" you. They shouldn't expect you to keep pace with every fitness activity they have mastered. You simply won't be able to. That's OK. Remember, the effort and desire you show your partner will probably go just as far toward creating a tighter bond as would crossing the finish line together.

At first, you may have to focus on forms of physical exercise you can handle on your own, so as to methodically close the gap between your fitness levels. Still, there's so much emotional value to couples exercising together, so make sure to strike a compromise and start making a list of shared fitness activities you'll both enjoy. Now, "shared" doesn't necessarily mean that you have to engage in identical exercises or activities. You can certainly go to the gym and work on weights while the other takes a Zumba class. You might go together to the local high school track, where you briskly walk while your partner keeps up his usual six-minute mile pace. The idea is that on some level, there is a sense of togetherness in your campaign for better health and fitness. Eventually, you'll want to have at least a few fitness activities you both love doing together. At that point, fitness becomes as much of a "date" as it is the pursuit of individual health.

FOOD FOR THOUGHT: Exercise can make you more attractive to your partner at a very primal level. It creates physiological arousal like sweaty hands, racing pulse, and shortness of breath, mirroring the thrill of romantic attraction ("Five Studies Show Why Couples Who Sweat Together Stay Together," *Psychology Today*, January 10, 2014).

F.I.D. AND FITNESS

Once you zero in on a few modes of exercise you both truly enjoy doing together, there's still the matter of F.I.D. and that fickle thing called "love metabolism." This is the second level of compromise for a couple. You now both agree on a particular physical activity you'd like to try together, but you have yet to figure out how often is enough, how long is good, and how intense it should be.

Let's suppose that you both make a commitment to better fitness by swimming laps at the local recreation center and that one of you is in much better shape than the other. First, you have to look at the frequency. Now, finding the sweet-spot for frequency is somewhat a matter of maximizing health benefits. A person in better shape will by necessity need to go crank up some variable of F.I.D., whether it's the frequency, intensity or duration. But whatever your fitness level, we suggest going together as often as possible because of the psychological benefits, alone. The simple acts of planning and following through consistently on that plan have a way of establishing a sense of "couples-culture." In other words, the routine just turns into one of those things you do as a couple that signals your "togetherness." It's the kind of thing that has other couples saying, "Did you know they go swimming together *three mornings a week?*"

FOOD FOR THOUGHT: Couples that have a shared fitness goal boost the quality of their romantic relationship and increase their happiness ("Five Studies Show Why Couples Who Sweat Together Stay Together," *Psychology Today*, January 10, 2014).

Still, the fact that you go swimming often in no way implies you can keep up with your partner. This is where we get into the variables of duration and intensity. Let's assume you're the lesser swimmer of the two. No problem, as there are several ways to compromise. Say your partner's cardiovascular fitness level is such that he can do laps for 30 minutes straight, while you're lucky to do six laps at a time, swimming for no more than 15 minutes total (duration). Let's also assume he needs to swim much faster than you to feel the burn. He keeps going at his wicked pace while you find yourself gassed, needing frequent breaks.

So what? Swimming is, after all, an individual endeavor at its core. We've not aware of any couples that have successfully held hands or carried on a conversation while free-styling across a body of water. Let your partner do his thing, while you make your frequent stops, resting easy in the knowledge that you're doing what you can to improve your health and your relationship. When it gets to be too much for you, drift over to the other area of the pool and do some resistance training in the water while he goes on and on like the aquatic Forrest Gump that he is. Remember, it's the element of synergy—that spirit of cooperation and connection—that creates the bond, not so much the act of moving lock-step with your partner. You're showing up. You're making the effort. You're together!

GETTING STARTED

It can take some time, patience, and sacrifice for many couples to find a fitness groove that works for both partners. With that in mind, we'll help get you started on the road to fitness fidelity by listing some "exercise dates" that you may find enjoyable:

1. Walking—This works for just about anyone who can put one foot in front of the other. Go as slow or as fast as you'd like. What's nice about this option is that you can actually talk with one another. Think about it. Two forms of bonding in one! If you're looking for ways to streamline your efforts toward greater intimacy, this might be your ticket.

2. Cycling—this has the benefit of fitting nicely at any point along the fitness intensity spectrum. You can enjoy some basic, boardwalk style cruising down a side walk, adventure together down a mountain trail, or don spandex and tackle a steep mountain pass on touring bikes. You can also ride side-by-side on stationary bikes in a "spinning" class.

3. Jogging/sprinting/stair-climbing—all have built-in intensity variables to suit anyone's needs. If you go with your partner to your local high school track and field, you can knock out all three.

4. Hiking—There are trails just about everywhere to accommodate just about every fitness level. We especially endorse this one! It gets you out into nature, works your heart and leg muscles, and gives you plenty of opportunity to chat.

5. Kayaking/canoeing—This is particularly beneficial when you use a two-man kayak or canoe. It's a great exercise in cooperation, communication, and coordination. Once you get in synch with one another and start moving as one, it's a truly great feeling.

6. Swimming—It's low impact and highly efficient. It works muscles throughout the body and gets the heart pumping like few other aerobic activities. As we said, the only downside is that it's inherently

an individual pursuit (unless you and your partner are synchronized swimmers). Still, we highly recommend it.

7. Co-ed sports teams—This option can be rigorous (soccer), moderate (softball), or more on the sedentary side (league bowling). Team sports certainly offer some health and relationship benefits, but because of their highly "social" nature, they may not work to give you the quality, one-on-one exercise time you need. While we recognize how much fun you can have, we also recommend that team sports not be your only mode of exercising together.

8. Formal aerobic exercise classes—like team sports, these are done in groups and therefore limit the possibility for intimate social interaction. However, the two of you tackling and mastering a challenging workout, such as CrossFit, Zumba®, or BodyPump™, could really give you a sense of accomplishment as a couple.

9. Racquet sports: Many racquet sports are especially built for two (it's no accident the sport of tennis uses the term "love" instead of "zero"). Like other activities, tennis can be as relaxing or as intensely competitive as you prefer. This goes for racquetball, squash and pickle ball, too.

10. Dancing: What could be more romantic? Depending on the nature of your dancing, it can be great cardiovascular exercise, as well. Whether you're moving around gracefully to a ballroom waltz or throwing each other around the room to big band swing, you can easily find a modality that both physically challenges you and rekindles a little passion.

FOOD FOR THOUGHT: *Couples Workouts for Health and Happiness* is Gina's new series of workout DVDs designed especially for you to do with your partner. There are three DVDs in the series (*Flexibility, Strength, Cardio*), each one offering three different levels of difficulty. Get your copy today at Amazon.com!

Couple's Quiz: FITNESS

Answer each question by rating the variable of F.I.D. using a number from the scale below. Then ask your partner to do the same. Later, you'll add the total scores to a worksheet in the concluding chapter.

> How satisfied are you with the level of
> **PHYSICAL ACTIVITY** in your relationship?

For you . . .

SUBJECT	FREQUENCY	INTENSITY	DURATION	SCORE
Fitness				

For your partner . . .

SUBJECT	FREQUENCY	INTENSITY	DURATION	SCORE
Fitness				

Rating Scale
5 = very satisfied; **4** = satisfied; **3** = somewhat satisfied;
2 = somewhat dissatisfied; **1** = dissatisfied; **0** = very dissatisfied

Total Score Key
0–5 = Needs a lot of work; **6–10** = Needs some attention; **11–15** = Doing well

CHAPTER 17

Sharing Life Through Shared Activities

Of course, not everything you enjoy doing together will revolve around physical activity. We hope you have several non-fitness hobbies, interests or recreational activities that you both enjoy pursuing together. Then again, perhaps you're one of those couples that struggle to find mutually enjoyable pursuits of any kind. Does one of you hunger to go places and do things, while the other is content to work on puzzles from the comfortable perch of an easy-chair? Neither is inherently "wrong," mind you. It's the love-metabolic mismatching that causes problems. When there are few or no shared interests, it really limits what you can talk about and experience together. The more you share, both in word and deed, the more likely you are to feel connected and fulfilled. If all that you share are the mundane details of life (such as errands, chores, meals, or family gatherings), chances are your relationship could be craving a real spark.

That missing spark comes in the form of the neurotransmitter dopamine, in fact. Research shows that the way people can keep manufacturing and feeding off of this most natural "love-happy chemical" is by finding new and exciting things to do together. As couples expand their recreational horizons and develop new interests, they experience those happy feelings and forge new bonds.

This is exactly what happened for an elderly woman we knew. Her story didn't start out so positive, though. She was never really close to her husband. They didn't have much to talk about or anything they truly loved doing together. They raised their kids and lived life. That was about it. Then came a little sports miracle that changed everything, just a short time before he passed away. It was 1980, the year the U.S. Olympic hockey team shocked the world by defeating the vaunted Soviet team in the semi-finals. The couple watched each game religiously, rooted for the team, and celebrated each victory all the way to the gold medal. It changed the feeling in their home and, for the first time, made her feel emotionally connected to her husband. True, it was only hockey, but it ultimately brought them closer and breathed life into a stagnate relationship.

For this woman, one shared interest made a huge difference. In our experience, however, one is not usually enough. That's why we routinely tell couples to try to find at least five things they love to do together. Now, it's likely you've partnered with someone who already enjoys some of the pursuits you do. Naturally, common interests are one of the reasons people come together in the first place. But if you're one of those couples that came together for other reasons and lack common interests, start going to work on this right away! Sit down together and start brainstorming activities, hobbies and interests. You may want to start with those that you already do individually. Is there a way you can get involved in something the other is doing, at least on some level? For example, if your partner happens to be a bird watcher and it's not really your thing, can you compromise by planning a day trip that features a kind of "bird-watching for dummies" tutorial, mixed with other attractions that better fit your interests? Who knows? After a nice outing with your partner, you might wind up being more interested in birds than you thought.

After you take inventory of what's already in your arsenal, you can start listing things that neither of you do on a regular basis. To help you organize your thoughts, it may be beneficial to think about activities in various categories. Here are several:

1. A few hours or under
2. Half-day
3. Whole-day
4. Weekend
5. Week-long or longer
6. Expensive
7. Inexpensive or cheap
8. Low-energy/sedentary
9. High-energy/active
10. Homebound
11. Out and about

With these in place, begin brainstorming hobbies/activities/interests and filing them into the categories you created. This will help you plan better in the future. When you need a shared activity to fill an open weekend, for example, you'll have a list of options ready to go. If you're both exhausted from being on the road for work or vacation, you'll have ready-made activities you can enjoy together from the comfort of your home. We have created a list below to help you get started. Once you have *yours* created, start prioritizing each item until you have your top five. Perhaps you'll end up with many more than that. More power to you!

FOOD FOR THOUGHT: The *Chicago Tribune* reports that couples who have shared hobbies have stronger marriages (August 30, 2015). They cite examples of couples who take cooking classes together, collect coins and join fantasy football leagues.

HERE'S OUR STARTER LIST, IN NO PARTICULAR ORDER:

- Books (reading out loud together or side-by-side), audio books, book clubs
- Live music, concerts, music festivals, karaoke
- Conventions and conferences
- Experiencing new restaurants, ethnic foods; food festivals; happy hours
- Museums, art galleries, science centers, planetariums
- Car shows, garden shows, pet shows, home shows
- Cooking classes, "beer school," confectionary classes
- Festivals, carnivals, and state and county fairs
- Professional, collegiate or high school sporting events
- Arts and crafts classes (e.g., painting or pottery making)
- Day-trips, nature drives, local sightseeing
- Domestic and international travel
- Card games, board games, video games
- Participation in civic organizations, charities, clubs (e.g., Rotary, Elks)
- Movies, television series, documentaries
- Wine-tasting tours and festivals
- Fishing, camping, hunting
- Recreational boating
- Parasailing, paragliding, hang-gliding, skydiving
- Snow skiing, snowshoeing, waterskiing, paddle-boarding, surfing
- Bungee jumping, zip-lining
- Stamp, coin, antique, and other types of collecting

Couple's Quiz: **SHARED ACTIVITIES**

Answer each question by rating the variable of F.I.D. using a number from the scale below. Then ask your partner to do the same. Later, you'll add the total scores to a worksheet in the concluding chapter.

How satisfied are you with the level of
SHARED ACTIVITY in your relationship?

For you . . .

SUBJECT	FREQUENCY	INTENSITY	DURATION	SCORE
Shared Activities				

For your partner . . .

SUBJECT	FREQUENCY	INTENSITY	DURATION	SCORE
Shared Activities				

Rating Scale
5 = very satisfied; **4** = satisfied; **3** = somewhat satisfied;
2 = somewhat dissatisfied; **1** = dissatisfied; **0** = very dissatisfied

Total Score Key
0–5 = Needs a lot of work; **6–10** = Needs some attention; **11–15** = Doing well

CHAPTER 18

Feeling Your Way Through Finances

They came from different worlds, as they say. He was from a small town, raised by conservative, practical-minded parents with little money to spare. She was from the city, where she went shopping nearly every day with her mother and enjoyed Sunday matinees at the movie theater. In spite of their divergent upbringings, loneliness and the longing for emotional security brought them together; it was a second marriage for each. On the night of their reception, they enjoyed their "first dance" as a married couple. She had requested the classic love ballad, Debby Boone's "You Light Up My Life." It was electric—the purest romantic energy they would ever experience as a couple. Unfortunately, but inevitably, things changed from there. Their mental wiring around finances was just too different. For years to come, she would sit there wondering where the spark went while he would sit there wondering why the electric bill was so high. It was ironic, if you think about it. Driven by the urge to save money, a man who once danced to "You Light Up My Life" spent his remaining years wandering the house in search of lights to *turn off!*

Our friend, Kathleen Cummins, would have been able to diagnose their problem right away. She is a senior vice-president and financial advisor with Morgan Stanley who works daily with couples. Kathleen knows from experience that there is generally one person in the relationship who plays the role of "spender," while the other assumes the role of "saver." As with other love-metabolic mismatches we've discussed up to this point, the financial kind can be very serious, indeed. In fact, it's well known that conflict around money is one of the leading causes of break-ups and divorce. Now, in a perfect world, you would have chosen someone from the get-go that shares your financial values. In theory, that would eliminate a lot of stress from the outset.

FOOD FOR THOUGHT: Money and sex consistently rank among the top two reasons why couples fight (Lisa Smith. "The No.1 Reason Why Couples Fight," on Investopedia.com).

But we don't always choose a mate based on the blasé foundation of financial philosophy, do we? Furthermore, it's not necessarily a bad thing to have the "spender-saver" as a working model for your relationship. Diversity in this way can serve as a type of checks and balances. Perhaps you need help tightening the belt while your partner needs help loosening his grip. Whatever the possible benefits to the saver/spender model, it's still quite a precarious situation. The fact is many couples fall into the extremes, which initiates a vicious cycle: The more you spend, the tighter your partner gets; the tighter your partner gets, the more you feel compelled to spend. At that point you have financial insanity, a place where financial decision-making is no longer governed by reason, but rather by anxiety.

That's how things got for Kevin and Rhonda, who sought couples counseling because of their weekly fights over finances. Try as they might, they just couldn't get on the same page because they looked at money so differently. One day in session, Kevin was particularly exasperated:

"Rhonda just spends so much money," he explained. "Every week I can see it from our online bank account. I see expenditures at the grocery store, the gas station, the community center, the Starbucks and the local shopping mall, not to mention all the checks she writes for the kids' activities. One time, she wrote checks for soccer, cheerleading camp and PTA dues, all in the same week. In fact, I don't think a day goes by that she doesn't spend money on something."

Rhonda quickly defended herself. "OK, I make a lot of purchases. A lot of small ones. So what? Kevin spends money on big ticket items that he doesn't even talk to me about first. One time I got home from work and, low and behold, we miraculously had a massive, plasma TV and a surround-sound speaker system set up in the family room. Oh, and he signed us up for Netflix and some other online movie subscription! I just couldn't believe he would spend all that money without talking to me first!"

Alarmed how the tables had been turned on him, Kevin vigorously fired back. "Rhonda, that TV and speaker system was on sale—that day only! It was the last one in stock. I got a killer deal on that whole setup! You know everyone in the house had been complaining about the way the volume was going out on the old TV. Plus, the kids can use the Netflix account to watch the History Channel for school projects. This is something we can all enjoy. I did this *for the family*!"

Rhonda scoffed sarcastically. "Oh, really? For the family? Just like the 'family' motorcycle you bought, the one the kids are afraid to ride with you? Or the 'family' boat we have sitting on the side of the house with expired tabs? Or the 'family' snow boards we only use twice a year?"

Yes, they were a "fun" couple, indeed. Never a dull moment in therapy. Unfortunately, their plight is all-too-common. Have you ever had similar kinds of financial arguments with your partner? If you're like most couples, you have. Of course, what you actually argue about and the reasons why you argue in the first place can vary. Have you ever worried about how you will get the bills paid while one of you is temporarily laid off? Have you had to devise creative solutions in order to pay for an unexpected expense, such as a broken furnace, leaky roof or bad radiator? Do you ever have disagreements over how to best save or invest your extra money? The list of financial challenges that can and will come up in a partnership are numerous.

As you might imagine, the way you view and approach money is significantly shaped by your personality and upbringing. If you were raised in a family that struggled and lived pay check to pay check, you may be more frugal with your finances. You might be more of a planner, anticipating monetary emergencies and allocating money to savings accordingly. Perhaps you're just wired to enjoy the "art" of finding a good deal—that thrill of getting the most for the least amount possible. If you grew up in a family in which money was either abundant or "appeared" to be abundant, you may find it quite natural to spend money more freely. Perhaps it's not the example of your parents, but rather an "easy come, easy go" financial philosophy you adopted that helps you avoid taking money too seriously.

How about a couple of counterintuitive possibilities where the opposite is true? If you were raised in a penny-pinching household as a child, you might want to spend lavishly as an adult. If you were fed with a silver spoon growing up, you might choose to follow a path of frugal living and charitable giving. It can and does happen. The larger point here is that much of how we react to money doesn't have to do with the actual amount of money we possess. It's often much more an issue of how we "feel" about money that drives our financial attitudes and habits.

Let's go back to Kevin and Rhonda for a moment. From a love-metabolic perspective, it's not so hard to understand how they reached this volatile impasse. You can already see the F.I.D. variables at play in their dialogue above. Let's start with "frequency." Rhonda was the one who managed the household. As manager of household *needs*, she was also the default manager of household *funds*. As she only worked part time, she had more time to spare and thus more time to shop than Kevin did. Naturally, the number of transactions she made far outnumbered Kevin's. If Kevin had been a single-dad solely responsible for his children, it would be his name on all those checks! But Kevin wasn't seeing things from that point of view. Instead, he saw all the debits in his checking account and became frustrated by the frequency of expenditures. To him, it "felt" like her spending was out of control, when it really wasn't.

While it's true that house managers spend money more often (frequency), it's not necessarily true that they spend more extravagantly (intensity). Sometimes the one that makes fewer transactions (in this case, Kevin) is the one who makes most of the really big purchases. We're not picking on either gender, here. Although men tend to make fewer but bigger purchases (such as cars, boats or golf clubs), women have also been known to drop a pretty penny on jewelry, designer handbags, and other luxuries. It goes both ways. Then there are those big ticket items that entice either gender equally, such as vacations, furniture for the house, or large landscaping projects for the yard. Regardless of gender, what really matters is that there's usually one in the relationship who wants the purchase more than the other, which has the potential to cause bitterness in the partner who isn't as interested.

Lastly (but loosely), we'll add the variable of "duration" to the mix. For the purposes of this chapter, we'll consider "duration" as how much time, consideration and thought you put into your spending habits. Do you shop for weeks looking for just the perfect winter coat? Do you look online, in the department stores, and at the outlet malls? Do you wait until it goes on sale, then snatch it up feeling proud of how long you held out? Or are you an impulse buyer? Do you see something that you love and find it too hard to resist? Maybe you didn't *really* need it or it wasn't *really* in your budget, but the deal was just too good to pass up and you snagged it. *Duration* can also apply to your saving trends. Have you been methodically saving money for years since you got married or graduated from college? On the contrary, is it something you are still planning to do—*someday*? Are you one of those financial procrastinators who puts off opening up your mail and paying bills? In short, some people take their time when it comes to financial matters while others would rather get in and get out.

MAKE A PLAN

Money might make the world go round, but it also carries emotional baggage. As a couple, you have to learn to see past the numbers and start embracing the emotional aspects of your finances. For starters, we recommend you sit down and identify your priorities and values. Don't mind-read. You may think that creating a college savings accounts for the children is a top priority, but your partner may not. Discuss the way you think and feel about spending, saving, investing and donating. Try to find common values, build on them, and then work to understand how your partner's point of view differs. If you just can't agree on certain financial priorities or practices, you might consider creating both joint and individual bank accounts. That way you can divide certain funds that can be used exclusively as each partner desires. We have seen this work successfully with couples who want to support different charities or pursue expensive, individual hobbies.

Next, create a budget together. Look at your regular income and fixed expenses. Get a clear picture of what it takes to meet basic needs. After that, you can decide what to do with expendable income. Put your optional expenditures in categories of "most important," "moderately important," and "least important." This will help you separate the "needs" from the "wants." Having this kind of discussion can evoke some strong feelings. Try your best to stay cool and allow an open discussion, the kind in which all things are on the table to examine.

FOOD FOR THOUGHT: According to a *Money® Magazine* survey by James E. McWhinney, couples fight about money twice as much as they fight about sex ("Top 6 Marriage-Killing Money Issues" on Investopedia.com).

Once you create your budget, get together each week to briefly note upcoming expenses, decide who will handle them, review your bank account, and get a jump on paying bills. We advise couples do this on Saturday or Sunday. Taking 15 minutes to get on the same page with each other can go a long way to keeping financial anxieties in check. Then set up a time once a month to review the budget. Life has a way of throwing financial curveballs and regular reviews will allow you to make needed adjustments to keep your budget current. Commit to quarterly reviews, as well. Are you meeting your goals of saving, investing or paying off your debts? If not, it's a great time to revise goals to be more realistic, find more strategic ways to cut expenses, and consider creative ways to open up alternative streams of income.

At the end of the year, sit down and review your progress over the previous year. Did you accomplish your goals? Were you able to compromise and work successfully together? Did you make strides in accommodating each other's unique outlook on money? Once you're done looking back, look ahead with hope to a year of even greater cooperation, collaboration, and accomplishment. As part of that collaboration, we strongly recommend that you create a few simple "rules of the relationship" about spending. Some examples we like are:

1. Never purchase something over $50 that's not on the budget before running it by your partner first.

2. Allow surprise gifts to each other (Valentine's Day, Father's Day, etc.) but within a set dollar amount you both are comfortable with.

3. Make sure both partners are getting some "fun items" they enjoy. You don't need to be as rigid as "one guy's golf weekend with his buddies = one girlfriend's spa day away," but you get the idea.

4. Never hide money or keep secrets about other accounts. Money holds power and it should never be used to manipulate or control one another.

5. Don't loan or give money away to friends or family members without talking to your partner about it first. Their input may help you see the situation in a different way.

6. Never lie about your expenditures. If you do, come clean right away. The truth usually has a way of coming out in the end and it will cost you!

7. After you're finished making your rules, try the couples exercise below (adapted from *1001 Questions to Ask Before You Get Married*, Monica Mendez Leahy, McGraw-Hill, 2004) designed to help you clarify your financial values. We think you'll not only find it helpful, you'll have some fun doing it. Good luck!

ACTIVITY: FINANCIAL VALUES

Instructions: Assume that circumstances are forcing you to cut expenses dramatically. Working separately, take a look at the list of expenses below and cross out expenses you're willing to eliminate. Then circles expenses you "can't live without." Once you're both finished, compare your decisions and then compromise to create a list of only five shared expenses.

- Cable TV
- A second car
- Full-coverage auto insurance
- Out-of-town vacations
- Going out to movies
- Concerts or professional sporting events
- Dining out
- Ordering take-out meals or fast food
- Buying snacks or other nonessential food items
- Daily stops to coffee shops
- Buying lunch at work
- Weekly outings with friends

- Birthday gifts for friends or family
- Having and maintaining a pet or pets
- Gym membership or personal trainer
- Club membership dues or expenses
- Paying more than the minimum due on monthly bills
- Rented storage space
- Visiting amusement parks or other attractions
- Contributions to church or charities
- Expenses incurred by a hobby
- Alcoholic beverages
- Cigarettes or cigars
- Child's private schooling, lessons, or tutors
- Schooling or classes taken by you or your spouse
- Home repair projects
- Lottery tickets or other gaming activities
- Sending or loaning money to relatives
- Internet access charges
- Magazine and newspaper subscriptions
- Cell phones
- Saving for retirement (401(k), IRA, or other)
- Contributions towards a college savings fund
- Lawn and garden service
- Housekeeper or cleaning service
- Daycare or nanny
- Serviced car wash
- Oil changes
- Expensive haircuts or hair treatments
- Beauty treatments (manicures, waxing, etc.)
- Massages or chiropractic care
- Purchases of clothes or shoes
- Dry cleaning

Couple's Quiz: FINANCES

Answer each question by rating the variable of F.I.D. using a number from the scale below. Then ask your partner to do the same. Later, you'll add the total scores to a worksheet in the concluding chapter.

How much stress does **MONEY** cause in your relationship?

For you . . .

SUBJECT	FREQUENCY	INTENSITY	DURATION	SCORE
Finances				

For your partner . . .

SUBJECT	FREQUENCY	INTENSITY	DURATION	SCORE
Finances				

Rating Scale
5 = negligible stress; **4** = a little stress; **3** = some stress;
2 = moderate stress; **1** = considerable stress; **0** = overwhelming stress

Total Score Key
0–5 = Needs a lot of work; **6–10** = Needs some attention; **11–15** = Doing well

CHAPTER 19

Getting Your Fill by Giving Back

Allison's eyes flew wide open as she entered the doorway to her deluxe suite and took in the beauty and splendor of the décor. Her husband, Blaine, followed behind her but froze for a moment with his mouth slightly agape, heavy bags still in hand. It was easily the most well-appointed, luxurious room they had ever reserved. Allison moved quickly past the beautiful furnishings, making a beeline for the patio window. She threw back the curtains, opened all the blinds, and felt the tropical light cascade into the room. After a deep breath and a long, pleasant sigh, she opened her eyes, looked back toward Blaine, and motioned for him to follow her out on to their 15th story balcony.

The view was simply spectacular! There were palms, people, and immaculate landscaping far below. There were pools, fountains, pathways and cozy gazebos. White, sandy shores and the Pacific Ocean in all its splendor stood off to the right. Allison's gaze then slowly shifted east in the direction of what *really* brought them back to Puerto Vallarta, Mexico. She peered into the distance and made a sweeping motion with her pointed finger, saying, "Those kids are somewhere out there, Blaine! Can't wait to see them."

"Yep," he answered, "It's gonna feel good to get over there again." They smiled, embraced, and left the balcony hand in hand to unpack their bags and unwind. Shortly they would be eating at one of their favorite restaurants, dancing at the nightclub, and enjoying a moonlight walk on the beach. But as much as they looked forward to all these things, that's not why they came back. It wasn't the luxury, the relaxation, or the sunshine that made them choose this location for the third year in a row. It was those kids in the nearby orphanage.

Several years ago, Allison and Blaine stumbled upon an opportunity to "give back while kicking back," a concept that is gaining some traction in the travel industry. The term "voluntourism" is used by some to describe the new trend. Their introduction came when a friend, who was intimately familiar with the humanitarian needs in the area, suggested they take a day out of their vacation to visit the nearby orphanage. He also had other suggestions for ways in which they could serve in the local community, even if it were only for a few hours. Allison and Blaine were a little hesitant at first, worrying some about personal safety, the possibility of getting lost, and running into language barriers. In truth, they were more uncomfortable about the prospect of souring their taste of paradise by facing the ugly realities just around the corner. Yes, they knew it was there, but what could they *really* do about it? Besides, they were there to relax, decompress and strengthen their relationship, not to save the world. There would be time and opportunity to do their share once they returned to the daily grind of life back home.

After mulling it over, though, Allison had a change of heart and prevailed on Blaine to give it a try with her. They planned for a couple of hours at most. But after meeting, playing with, and helping to care for many of the orphaned children, a couple of hours turned into half a day. Even after they returned to the resort, they were so moved by the experience—so touched by a sense of compassion and the feeling of gratitude for all they had in life, most of all each other—that they went back the next day to make a financial donation to the orphanage. The next year they returned, they did much of the same, spending even more time than before. Their associations there led them to other nearby opportunities to serve, as well. By the end of their trip that second year, they realized how much these little sacrifices to give back had transformed their entire concept of "vacationing," giving them a profound sense of purpose and meaning they had not known before when traveling together. By connecting to others in need, they connected with each other in a way they never had before on *any* vacation.

FOOD FOR THOUGHT: People who give back are happier, healthier and live longer:

- *Older adults who volunteer at least 200 hours per year are 40% less likely to develop high blood pressure*
- *Those who volunteer have 22% lower mortality than those who do not*
- *Volunteers show improved well-being and more satisfaction with life*
- *Volunteers have less depression*
- *Studies suggest that volunteers have better mental health and cognitive function*

("People Who Volunteer May Be Happier, Healthier, and Live Longer," by Anthony Rivas, August 25, 2013, on www.medicaldaily.com)

At its core, the entire concept of voluntourism is all about capturing and spreading happiness. In our practices, we understand that helping patients get better is not merely an exercise in reducing such symptoms as depression and anxiety; it's also the art of helping them discover what makes them *happy*. Researchers in the field of positive psychology, a school of psychology concerned with human happiness, have been conducting studies around the world for a few decades now. What's quite interesting about the findings is that no matter who you are or where you live—whether you're a Wall Street investment banker in Manhattan or a tribal chief in the bush of Sub-Saharan Africa—there are a few universal truths about what can and can't produce happiness. No surprise, *giving back* is something that makes everyone happy.

Alfred Adler, an understudy of Sigmund Freud who emphasized the therapeutic necessity for human social interaction, affectionately talked about *giving back* in terms of "community feeling" and "social interest." Another theorist who also studied under Freud, Erik Erikson, described the idea in connection with an important developmental life stage he called, "Generativity versus Stagnation." In this stage, people 40 to 65 years old either work to make the world a little better or become selfishly disconnected and dissatisfied. Whatever you choose to call it, the act of giving back is one of the primary factors in creating human happiness. We're happier when we feel that our very existence has meaning and purpose beyond daily survival, that we belong to something larger than ourselves, and that what we do can leave a lasting footprint for good in this world.

While we know that giving back is as powerful a tool for generating happiness for couples as it is for individuals, romantic partners don't always share the same passion and drive. In other words, their love metabolic rates burn differently when it comes to charitable pursuits. Sometimes it's as simple as one having it in his or her DNA, seemingly, while the other just isn't interested—as if the light hasn't been turned on yet. Suffice it to say, this kind of couple could experience some significant love-metabolic drift. In other partnerships, each shares the same basic desire to give back, but one is usually more instinctively motivated and has a much more fully developed idea of how often, how long, and how much he or she wants to give back. Even if you *did* share the same appetite for giving back, you might not share the same charitable interests. Perhaps you feel compelled to spend your time, money and energy in very different ways than your partner does. That's OK! However you choose to make your mark, giving back makes you happier, and a happier you makes a happier romantic partner.

As Allison and Blaine discovered, your happiness and fulfillment as a couple can increase exponentially if you find ways to volunteer that both of you can embrace and enjoy. That's the real objective, here: The positive effects on your relationship are significant. Assuming you do find charitable pursuits that you can agree on, then F.I.D. comes into play. How often are you comfortable volunteering? How much time are you willing to commit to each event or project? How willing are you to tackle physically demanding or emotionally challenging pursuits? Let's be honest. There's a big difference between taking registrations at a local charity's annual "fun run" and committing to three full days a week working with inmates at a high-security prison. Sure, these examples fall on polar opposite ends of the F.I.D. spectrum, but you get the point!

There is much to discuss and decide as you consider how to move forward. You might conclude, for example, that reading to children at the library is something you both really enjoy. That's a good start. The only problem is that your partner wants to commit to five evenings a week while you see it as more of a twice-a-month endeavor. Or perhaps you both agree that you would like to travel to a developing country to help a community with their basic needs, but your idea of "helping" includes things like vaccinating children while your partner is planning to bust out the heavy tools and start framing houses. As with any attempt to bridge your love-metabolic gaps, you'll have to communicate and compromise along the way.

Remember, the goal isn't necessarily to engage in the same volunteer activity as the other. You can certainly work with medical supplies while your partner hefts two-by-fours, as in the case above. You made the trip together, you're serving in parallel capacities, and you're sharing the entire experience. If you're the couple volunteering at the library, there's nothing wrong with your partner putting to use their extra stamina and will by volunteering a couple of more days a week than you. At least you have the shared experience of reading to kids. Your partner will still feel in synch with you on the days you serve together and will know you can fully relate when he or she recounts stories from the days you're *not there*. So, by all means, don't let your love of giving back be hindered by some tedious discrepancy in F.I.D. If you happen to have more determination, spare time, interest, or wherewithal than your partner, you can always do a little more on your own to fill the need to give back.

The message is clear: *Get together* and decide how to *give back together*! We fully understand that not every couple is in the position to do as Allison and Blaine, who have the means to travel to exotic, international destinations. Thankfully, you don't have to go far away to get close to those in need. You don't need money, either—just a little time, a big heart, and a willing hand. To help you get started, we've outlined some volunteer categories, from small and simple to extravagant and expensive. Start by identifying categories that work best for you right now—the kinds of accessible volunteer opportunities you can get to work on right away. From there, you can begin to make a list of specific charitable activities that you both find appealing. You might even decide to rate them with one, two or three stars, according to how compelling, feasible, or fitting each one is.

Try not to limit yourself. This exercise is intended to open your mind to new volunteer possibilities as a couple. If, for example, one of you dreams of travelling to Bangkok, Thailand, for a two-week humanitarian excursion to work with victims of human trafficking, don't rule it out right away. Put it on your volunteer "bucket list" instead and consider how you might plan and save for it. In the meantime, you might find opportunities to help locally. You can actually help victims much closer to home, which in turn will give you valuable experience and expertise that will come in handy later in Thailand. As we have discovered, if you want something badly enough, you can usually find ways to make it happen. Set the intention, set your sights, and doors will open for you.

LIST OF CHARITABLE CATEGORIES:

1. Neighborhoods—Perhaps the most basic but effective way you can give back is to care for those nearest you. Chances are there is a senior or a single mom in need of support only a few blocks away. Assisting friends and neighbors with simple household repairs, providing them with meals when they are sick, or simply sitting down to provide some companionship and conversation are the kinds of charitable acts anyone can reasonably do.

2. Towns and cities—Most municipalities have volunteer committees that work to clean up local parks, repave trails, replenish food banks, or raise money for local causes. Additionally, you can often find opportunities to volunteer within your place of worship or at the school your children or grandchildren attend. Parks and recreation departments are nearly always looking for volunteers willing to coach both boys' and girls' seasonal sports teams. We know couples who enjoy volunteering one day a month at their local soup kitchen. Do you have a soft spot for animals? Volunteer at your local Humane Society, PAWS, or other animal shelter.

3. Counties and states—Going beyond the borders of your city, you can still give back in several ways. You don't have to be a politician to help promote and pass important legislation, assist in protecting and improving county and state parks, or work to clean up roads and highways.

4. National charities—Who hasn't noticed the flood of pink ribbons and paraphernalia associated with the Susan G. Komen® Foundation and its fight against breast cancer? It's just one of thousands of 501c3's in the United States looking for willing volunteers. Have you lost a loved one to leukemia, Alzheimer's, Parkinson's, multiple sclerosis, or some other hideous disease? Such personal tragedies can give you the passion and determination that national charities are looking for in their volunteers. Most of these organizations plan walks, runs and other types of public awareness campaigns. The opportunities to give back are countless.

5. Going global—This kind of giving back takes more time and planning to undertake, but the adventures and experiences you can have as a couple are extraordinary! There are many international volunteer organizations, travel clubs and ministries that all work to help you give back to people of the world, especially in developing countries. You can travel to Africa to assist in medical or dental clinics, go to Central America to build schools and dig wells, or journey to Southeast Asia to volunteer at women's shelters. The opportunities are as boundless as the oceans you will cross to reach them.

SAMPLE LIST OF CHARITABLE ACTIVITIES BY CATEGORY:

Neighborhoods
- Clean up
- Preparing meals
- Lawn care
- Home repairs
- Block watch
- Outreach/social committees

Towns/Cities
- Food banks
- Trail and park clean up
- Assisted living centers
- School classroom volunteer
- Church service committees
- Library
- Animal shelter
- Homeless shelter
- Domestic violence shelter
- Soup kitchen

- City council meetings
- Hospital help

County/State
- Legislative support
- State park preservation
- Clean water initiatives
- Fish and animal protection

National
- Non-profits for disease treatment and prevention (diabetes, MS, Parkinson's, ALS, etc.)
- HIV foundations
- Wildlife conservation organizations
- Equipment and technology

Global
- Natural disaster relief
- Children's orphanages/hospitals
- Domestic violence/human trafficking shelters and safe houses
- Basic need support (wells for drinking water, drainage, irrigation)
- Teaching and mentoring people in developing countries (reproductive health, computer technology, disease prevention, etc.)
- Medical/dental/vision clinics (supplies and labor support)
- Building projects (framing, roofing, painting, etc.)
  - Schools
  - Churches
  - Homes
  - Community centers
  - Shelters
  - Hospitals
- Sanitation projects (dump sites, cleaning polluted air and water)

Couple's Quiz: **GIVING BACK**

Answer each question by rating the variable of F.I.D. using a number from the scale below. Then ask your partner to do the same. Later, you'll add the total scores to a worksheet in the concluding chapter.

> How satisfied are you with your efforts as a
> couple to **GIVE BACK** to those in need?

For you . . .

SUBJECT	FREQUENCY	INTENSITY	DURATION	SCORE
Giving Back				

For your partner . . .

SUBJECT	FREQUENCY	INTENSITY	DURATION	SCORE
Giving Back				

Rating Scale
5 = very satisfied; **4** = satisfied; **3** = somewhat satisfied;
2 = somewhat dissatisfied; **1** = dissatisfied; **0** = very dissatisfied

Total Score Key
0–5 = Needs a lot of work; **6–10** = Needs some attention; **11–15** = Doing well

CHAPTER 20

Conclusion: Making the Most of *Love Metabolism*

Congratulations! You've made it to the final course of what we hope has been a smorgasbord of useful information. Please don't expect a fluffy dessert, though. Think of this chapter as a sampler platter of all that you've previously consumed. We'll start by offering a brief summary of each chapter. Then we'll walk you through the steps to help you organize and personalize the information that matters most to you. From there, you can start the journey of communication and compromise toward greater fulfillment in your relationship. We know that we've shared a lot with you! We also understand that you may have uncovered several areas of need in your relationship. Don't get discouraged by all these love-metabolic gaps. Focus instead on the hope that you can finally satisfy your hunger for love, one day at a time, one unmet need at a time. As we've said over and over, with enough desire, patience, and persistence, you'll get there—and the rewards will be incredible!

LOOKING BACK

In the first chapter of Part I, we introduced you to Jon and Jennifer, a couple who had a very specific unmet need: More communication. Jon was unsuccessful in his attempts to satisfy Jennifer's appetite for communication because he failed to take into account the three love-metabolic keys to meeting needs: How often, how long, how much (they talked often enough, but their conversations were too short-lived and superficial for Jennifer's liking). We then showed you how these three love-metabolic variables compare to the fitness industry's concept of F.I.D. (frequency, intensity, and duration).

From there, we explored in greater detail the topic of love metabolism and communication in chapters two and three. While satisfying hunger for communication is ultimately decided by individual preferences, it's also heavily influenced by gender. We reviewed some common male/female communication miscues, such as men's focus on *content* versus women's focus on *process,* women's need to be heard versus men's need to fix things, and male straight-talk versus female code-talking. Next, we "learned the burn" of communication by removing the gender lens and considering your romantic partner's unique needs as an individual. Whether through texting or emails, phone calls or cards, we demonstrated how communication needs to be tailor-made to fit your partner's preferences.

In chapter four, we changed our view from what the heart craves to what the heart *can't stomach*! One by one, we considered several forms of communication that many people have a difficult time digesting, including sarcasm, criticism, teasing, debate and—the worst of the worst—disengagement. In similar fashion, in chapter five we discussed how people have varying degrees of love-metabolic tolerance for conflict. We showed you how to get on the same page with your partner by asking specific questions and adapting your behaviors to match the answers. We talked about the challenges of defining conflict, identifying hot-button issues, and determining how much conflict is too much.

In chapter six, we tackled a big issue. While it's true that friends and family can support and strengthen a relationship, too much or too little interaction can just as quickly sink it. We considered several important love-metabolic factors that shape appetites for friends and family and read two compelling stories—one inspiring and one disastrous—to help you learn how to serve up family and friends in the right portions. Moving on from friends and families to ex-spouses, co-workers, and neighbors, we focused in chapter seven on how to create healthy social boundaries to safeguard your relationship from "outside threats." We shared stories that illuminated the danger of poorly defined boundaries and highlighted the value of open communication.

In Part II, we introduced you to the book, *The 5 Love Languages*, and showed you how the idea of love metabolism and F.I.D can effectively build on the book's foundation. We discussed how people's desire for "words of affirmation" are affected by several variables, including gender, self-esteem, family culture, and personal experiences in relationships. We gave you strategies to better understand and satisfy both your partner's need for affirming words and your own. In chapter 10, we focused on the love language, "Quality Time," and considered the very diverse ways people define "quality." We shared two contrasting stories, one involving a couple whose attempts to increase intimacy failed miserably in Las Vegas and the other showcasing a couple that got the balance right in Maui. Through these, we revealed how connection and intimacy are forged by being together often enough, for the right amount of time, and with the right degree of focus and attention on one another.

In chapter 11, we introduced you to the love language, "Receiving Gifts," and all the love-metabolic factors to consider when giving a gift to the one you love. Using the gift of flowers as an example, we demonstrated how the secret to creating the optimum love-response is in the love-metabolic details of gift-giving (i.e., how often to send flowers, on what occasions, what kind to send, how they should be delivered, and so on). In chapter 12, we examined "Acts of Service" and considered how reaching another's heart through service is only accomplished by truly learning what works for them.

Last but not least, we looked at the human need for touch in chapter 13 and considered the many variables that affect a person's appetite for physical affection. Whether it's hugging, holding hands, snuggling, or public displays of affection, it's important to get the frequency, intensity, and duration variables correct. Then for good measure, we had some fun looking at Valentine's Day—a day when all the love languages come together in a perfect storm of love-metabolic hits and misses. Through a comprehensive list of Valentine *do*s and *do not*s, we saw how cupid hits his target, first by using the correct love language and second by expressing that language in a way that truly satisfies your partner's hunger.

In Part III, we talked about how to trade in a sex-life that simmers for one that sizzles (chapter 15)! We took a look at all the phases of intimate contact—from flirting to foreplay to full-on skin to skin contact—and considered how and why appetites can vary so much. In the process, we emphasized the need for honest and open communication, compromise and exploration with your partner. In the F.I.D. and fitness chapter (16), we identified the benefits of getting into better shape as a couple. In similar fashion, we looked at hobbies, recreational pursuits, and other shared interests in chapter 17, considering ways to rise above your love-metabolic differences and get the most out of your "together-time." In chapter 18, we talked about the dangers of different perspectives on money and gave you tools to help you organize your financial priorities, goals and practices. Finally, we concentrated on the relationship-transforming power of giving back to those in need, whether at home or abroad (chapter 19).

PUTTING IT ALL TOGETHER

Now that we're done looking back, let's set our sights on the bright future ahead of you. It's time to make sense of all that you've learned. No doubt, you've uncovered a few unfulfilled needs to work on, but where should you start? More appropriately, *how* should you start? We've outlined the steps you need to follow below. Here we go . . .

Step 1

Go back to each couple's quiz you completed (found at the end of most chapters) and transfer the numbers for frequency, intensity, duration, and total score into the worksheet on the next page. Then have your partner do the same. Each of you do your own work.

Couple's Quiz Score Sheet (For you...)

SUBJECT-PART I	FREQUENCY	INTENSITY	DURATION	SCORE
Communication				
Sarcasm				
Criticism				
Teasing				
Debate				
Disengagement				
Conflict				
Family/Friends				
Fam/Friends 2				
Boundaries				

SUBJECT-PART II	FREQUENCY	INTENSITY	DURATION	SCORE
Words of Aff.				
Quality Time				
Gifts				
Acts of Service				
Touch				
SUBJECT-PART III	FREQUENCY	INTENSITY	DURATION	SCORE
Sex				
Fitness				
Shared Activities				
Finance				
Giving Back				

Couple's Quiz Score Sheet (For your partner...)

SUBJECT-PART I	FREQUENCY	INTENSITY	DURATION	SCORE
Communication				
Sarcasm				
Criticism				
Teasing				
Debate				
Disengagement				
Conflict				
Family/Friends				
Fam/Friends 2				
Boundaries				

SUBJECT-PART II	FREQUENCY	INTENSITY	DURATION	SCORE
Words of Aff.				
Quality Time				
Gifts				
Acts of Service				
Touch				
SUBJECT-PART III	**FREQUENCY**	**INTENSITY**	**DURATION**	**SCORE**
Sex				
Fitness				
Shared Activities				
Finance				
Giving Back				

Step 2

Do you remember the scoring key at the bottom of each couple's quiz? You'll be referring to it to identify the more significant problem areas in your relationship. For your convenience, here is the total scoring key again:

Total Score Key
0–5 = Needs a lot of work; **6–10** = Needs some attention; **11–15** = Doing well

Now, go back over each total score in the far right column and place a checkmark by any that fall in the 0—5 range. These are areas that obviously need the most work. Next, go back and put an asterisk (*) by any total scores in the 6—10 range. These areas need some work, but should take a back seat to those in the 0—5 range. Between the checkmarks and asterisks, you should have enough to work on. Remember you're only looking at the total scores in the far right column, not the individual scores under frequency, intensity, and duration.

Example (partial worksheet):

SUBJECT-PART I	FREQUENCY	INTENSITY	DURATION	SCORE
Communication	1	5	2	8 *
Teasing	4	3	4	11
Conflict	3	0	1	4 ✓
Boundaries	4	4	4	12
Sex	3	1	1	5 ✓

In the worksheet above, you would place a checkmark by the total scores for sex (5) and conflict (4). You would then place an asterisk next to the total score for communication (8).

Step 3

Now that you have identified your primary areas of need, it's time to have a dialogue with your partner. We strongly recommend that you have this conversation as part of a planned date. Go out together, have fun, and get the good juices going beforehand. Then come back to your home or some other comfortable place and start comparing notes. Once you're finished with the conversation, plan to cap off the evening with a relaxing, preferably mindless, activity that will help you unwind.

As you look at the scores, we fully realize that you might be anything but shocked. After getting this far in the book, we're sure your mind is already spinning with ideas of how things need to change. Still, there may be metabolic deficits you hadn't counted on until you really viewed all the scores side by side. For instance, let's suppose that you already knew you had a problem with conflict in your relationship, but only after considering each component of F.I.D. did you fully come to understand the true nature of the problem lies with the intensity of that conflict. Our hope is that this kind of analysis will allow you to better pin-point what variable of F.I.D. needs to be adjusted.

Once you settle in with your partner, start the conversation by sharing the check-marked scores. Do any of your problem areas line up with your partner's, by chance? Could it be that both of you feel the need most in the same area (e.g., quality time)? If so, perhaps you're both dissatisfied for very different reasons (e.g., you want to get out more often while your partner wants longer vacations).

Whatever the case, your main task here is to identify and communicate your preeminent, unmet need. What one area of need tops your list? What tops your partner's list? Talk openly and freely about it, but also try to be as specific as possible, using F.I.D. as your foundation. Providing details and examples will help your partner better understand just how and why you feel unfulfilled. Own your feelings and faults. Don't use blaming language or sweeping generalizations. Remember, this isn't about who's right and who's wrong. Try to approach the conversation with the kind of thoughtful, collaborative spirit it deserves.

Once both of you have had an opportunity to share your primary unmet needs, take a deep breath and gauge the feeling in the room. Are you energized? Motivated? Do you feel closer? Did the whole ordeal wear you out? Do you feel tense or defensive? If so, it's probably best to step away for a bit and get some fresh air. There's nothing wrong with scheduling a sequel. If all's good, then move on to your remaining check-marked problem areas, then share any scores you marked with an asterisk. By the end of the day you should have plenty to sleep on.

Regardless of how far you get in reviewing your scores, make sure you focus most of your energy on your primary, unmet need. This is key. Don't go too deep in one sitting. Take one baby step at a time. We're not just worried about overloading or discouraging you; we want to ensure you get the process down, issue by issue. If you nail the process, the outcomes will take care of themselves. Allow us to outline that process for you below:

Instructions for Couples Quiz Conversation

1. Each of you choose one unmet need to work on as a couple (1 each = 2 total)

2. As described previously, provide a detailed, F.I.D.-friendly explanation of how and why the need remains unfulfilled.

   Example: I feel strongly that we're connecting well enough in our communication. I think we chat often enough, but that's just it. We only chat. I just don't feel like we have good conversations—you know—the kind where our phones are put away, the TV's off, and we talk about something that matters.

3. Make suggestions as to how your partner can better satisfy your primary, unmet need/brainstorm solutions together.

   Example: It seems like the only time we get to talk is while we're busy running around the house or on the way to somewhere. I wonder if we could plan to have an early morning walk each day. That would give us a chance to really talk.

4. Compromise and make necessary accommodations as needed.

   Example: To make this work, we're going to have to get up earlier than usual. How about we move up our evening routine a half-hour to an hour. Do you think we could get everything wrapped up and be asleep by 10 p.m. each night instead of 11?

5. Put the plan into action and keep it in play (even if it takes some time to stick).

6. Schedule a time to get together at regular intervals to review progress and share feedback.

   Example: I love that we've been able to walk most mornings over the last two weeks. It's allowed us the space we need to relax and really talk. I still feel a little disconnected with all we've got going during the weekends, though. I'd love to figure out if there's something similar we can do to create some quality talk-time on the weekends, too, perhaps on Sunday nights before the next week begins.

7. Incorporate, adapt, perfect . . . . *repeat!*

There you have it! That's the recipe for creating positive change. Master this process and you're well on your way to a more fulfilling, satisfying relationship. As we said above, it's important that you focus on the process, not your problems. That said, take your primary unmet need, whatever it may be, and go to work on that one alone. See the process through until you make substantial progress. Starting small will not only help you become accustomed to the process, but it will give you the satisfaction of a victory early in the game! That sense of accomplishment will give you the energy you need to take on the rest of your unfulfilled needs.

FINAL THOUGHTS

So that's it. We've come to the conclusion of our labor of love, *Love Metabolism*—well, for now. Stay tuned. We have aspirations to produce more books in the love metabolism vein. More than anything, our hope is that this book has given *you* hope. Relationships are difficult. They are a lot of work. Sometimes they are excruciating. Still, we believe in love. As indescribable as it is—as intangible as it may be—there is nothing greater to live and work for. John Lennon once sang, "All you need is love." Possibly. We'll let the philosophers debate that one. But while we adore the sentiment, we think it would be more accurate to say, "All you need is love that's made to order, served on time, and guaranteed to satisfy." Even though this marks the end of *our* journey together, *your* journey toward greater satisfaction and fulfillment is just beginning. Whereas we once said, "bon appetite," we now say, *bon voyage*! May you have all the love in life you've dreamed of!

AUTHOR INFORMATION

Gina Guddat
www.ginaguddat.com
gina@ginaguddat.com
https://www.facebook.com/GinaGuddat?fref=ts
https://twitter.com/ginaguddat

Ray Anderson
www.rayandersoncounseling.com
ray@rayandersoncounseling.com

Follow *Love Metabolism* on Facebook, Twitter, and Instagram